IN DEFENSE OF GOVERNMENT

The Fall and Rise of Public Trust

JACOB WEISBERG

SCRIBNER

SCRIBNER
1230 Avenue of the Americas
New York, NY 10020

SCRIBNER and design are
trademarks of Simon & Schuster Inc.

Set in Adobe Granjon
Designed by Brooke Zimmer

Manufactured in the United States of America

1 3 5 7 9 10 8 6 4 2

Library of Congress Cataloging-in-Publication Data
Weisberg, Jacob.
In defense of government : the fall and rise of public trust /
Jacob Weisberg.
p. cm.
Includes index.
1. United States—Politics and government. 2. United States—
Economic policy. 3. United States—Social policy. 4. Democratic
Party (U.S.) 5. Republican Party (U.S. : 1854–) I. Title.
JK271.W377 1996
320.973—dc20 96-5987
CIP

ISBN 0-684-81604-0

In memory of my father,
Bernard Weisberg

CONTENTS

INTRODUCTION

A<small>T FIRST GLANCE</small>, Pamela Jackson's apartment looks like any ordinary place. Her living room is functionally appointed with cheap furniture: a black vinyl sofa, matching love seat, glass coffee table, and a TV. Everything appears fairly new. Adjacent to the living room is a perfectly immaculate galley kitchen. In each of two small adjoining rooms, the beds are neatly made. If not for the smattering of framed photographs, a child's drawings, houseplants, and stuffed animals, one might mistake this for a motel suite of above average cheerfulness. A walk around the two-story redbrick development in which the apartment is situated only exacerbates the pervasive sense of dull normality. Driving around the Chicago suburb of Palatine heightens it further.

But to Pamela Jackson, the apartment represents far more. To her, a clean, safe, affordable place to live still comes as such a surprise that it induces a kind of euphoria when she talks about it, some nine months after moving in. For her, a nondescript apartment in a middle-class neighborhood is the basis of a new life, vastly better than the one she knew before. It is a sanctuary, a safe haven from conditions so degraded that most of us can only imagine them. A slim, bright-eyed woman, wearing a sleeveless denim dress on a hot autumn day, Pam sits on the edge of her sofa and races, tripping over her words as she tries to explain what the apartment means to her: Here there are no crackheads trying to sell secondhand bus transfers for a quarter, no giant rats, random shootings, or playgrounds strewn with broken glass. Instead there's a good suburban school where her daughter is learning to play the clarinet, a parking lot where she walks without fear at night, and a landlord who responds promptly to the complaint of a leaky faucet.

Jackson told me her story when I visited her in 1995. For the first thirty years of her life, she lived in a variety of public housing projects and privately owned slum apartments on Chicago's South Side. At twenty, she got pregnant and gave birth to a daughter, Porshá. Porshá's father, to whom Pam wasn't married, soon left, and she went on public assistance. For the next nine years, she was in and out of work, in and out of apartments, on and off welfare. The father of her daughter sometimes works, she says, but he will quit a job sooner than pay child support.

Poverty and danger turned mother and daughter into refugees in the city. Before moving to Palatine, they lived with the family of Pam's brother at Seventy-sixth and Union, sleeping on a sofa in the living room. Though she had a full-time job at Woolworth's, Pam couldn't afford a place of her own, even in a marginal neighborhood. In the last few years the area where she lived with her brother has gone from bad to intolerable. Seventy-ninth is "the street that never sleeps," Jackson says, with young men standing on the corner dealing drugs "all night, in every kind of weather." After getting off work at ten o'clock, she would have to cross that street to pick up Porshá at her baby-sitter's. Porshá's school, at Sixty-third and Dulles, was in a similarly menacing precinct, "with people hanging out under the El station, gangs and drug dealers," she says. Parkway Gardens, a blighted housing project, was the school's backyard. "On Sixty-second Street anything can happen," Pam says. Although reconciled to a measure of risk herself, she was afraid for Porshá. "I wanted some stability in my daughter's life," she says.

When, after a long struggle to get it, Pam moved to her new place in Palatine, the first thing she did was take off all of her clothes. "I never felt I could walk around, you know, free before. My daughter asked, 'Mama, why you walking around without any clothes?' Where I was you just don't have the freedom." They moved in on December 17, 1994. Jackson decided the apartment was her Christmas gift and got a small tree. A few months later, she bought herself a set of living room furniture as a birthday present.

The initial adjustment to life in an almost entirely white suburb was not easy for mother or daughter. When she began third grade at Stuart R. Paddock, an all-white public school, Porshá experienced what her mother describes as "culture shock." Though ordinarily lively and engaged, she clammed up in class. "All these white people—I just don't know what to say," Porshá told her mother, who says, "Now she's well adjusted. She interacts. She's doing wonderful." Porshá counts as her three best friends Jennifer, Cristina, and Tiffany—"Tiffany's a little white girl!" Pam exclaims, bursting into laughter. At her new school, Porshá has homework every day including Fridays. Now in fourth grade, she stays late for an optional course in composition. "You don't do that in the city," her mother says. Pam also appreciates that the school keeps close track of absences and invites parents to participate in a variety of school functions. "I like the school because they are involved. It's like a close-knit family," she says.

Pam herself expected to encounter rudeness if not worse from whites in Palatine. She was frightened the first time a police car pulled her over, because of stories she'd heard about blacks being beaten and harassed in the suburbs. But the officer was polite and friendly; he just wanted to warn her that one of her taillights was out. Now she says that as a single woman she appreciates the police cars she sees on patrol around her complex. As for her white neighbors, Pam says they "are friendlier than some blacks. They say 'Good morning' to you." Jackson likes other things about Palatine, such as the shopping. "You find things I don't find in the city," she says. "If you spending your money, they want to please you." Though afraid to drive on the expressway at first, she has gotten used to it and says she no longer minds commuting to her job in the city. "Call me a suburbanite," she says.

The comfort and calm of her new life have encouraged Jackson to think about her future in a way she never could before. Porshá has promised her mother that she will try college for at least a year when the time comes. And when her daughter is a bit older and her car is paid off, Pam would like to try college herself. Her other ambition is to own a home someday—in the suburbs. "If we do move again, I'm not going back to the city," she says. "The more I'm out here, the more I like it."

An unfashionable entity called big government made Pam Jackson's apartment possible. How exactly is a complicated story. It begins with a woman named Dorothy Gautreaux (pronounced "Guh-tro"), who lived, in the 1960s, in the Altgeld-Murray Homes, one of the many high-rise housing horrors built on Chicago's South Side between the late 1940s and the mid-1960s. From the start, Chicago's public housing was completely segregated and isolated from the rest of the city. White aldermen made sure that projects went up only in black neighborhoods, though it meant no subsidized housing would go to their constituents. Even today, the Chicago Housing Authority has no white tenants to speak of except in developments reserved for senior citizens. Altgeld-Murray, where Dorothy Gautreaux lived with her five children, was statistically the poorest of Chicago's all-black housing projects, the lowest circle of its high-rise hell.

Gautreaux was, however, an instinctive betterer who refused to accept the dismal circumstances in which her family found itself. Like her wealthier suburban counterparts, she helped organize Boy Scout and Girl Scout troops in her neighborhood, joined the PTA, and founded the Altgeld-Murray Parents Council to protest the poor quality of the schools that served the project. Her activism coincided with the civil rights movement in the early 1960s, and as that struggle gained momentum, Gautreaux became her group's representative inside the Coordinating

Council of Community Organizations, the movement's main vehicle in Chicago. In the sometimes raucous atmosphere of those times, Gautreaux was known as an island of patience and good sense. As Harold Baron, who worked for the Chicago chapter of the Urban League, recalled in a memoir about her, "When discussion became stymied over abstract principles or personalities, she punctured the posturing by quietly stating what she and her small band of tenant organizers were going to do."

Until 1965 Gautreaux and the CCCO concentrated on the issue of education. But that year, when Martin Luther King, Jr., came to Chicago, the movement's focus shifted to ending slums and creating open housing in the city King called the most segregated in the world. On one of his visits to Chicago, King went with Gautreaux to the Altgeld-Murray Homes for a rally. After that, Gautreaux became the informal representative not just of her project but of all public housing tenants inside the civil rights movement. King and his followers marched in some of the most segregated and hostile neighborhoods of the city, demanding that they open themselves to blacks. The marchers were pelted with stones, bottles, and garbage. In Marquette Park, King was hit in the head by a rock and knocked to the ground. He told a reporter: "If some of us have to die, then we will die."

King's followers opposed the Chicago Housing Authority's plan to build more segregated projects on the old model. They enlisted the ACLU to file a lawsuit to prevent the construction of more high-rise ghetto housing, on the grounds that it violated the equal protection clause of the Constitution and provisions of the 1964 Civil Rights Act. Dorothy Gautreaux was the first named plaintiff in the class action suit, which was lodged in 1966 against both the CHA and the U.S. Department of Housing and Urban Development. My father was one of the lawyers who prosecuted the suit.

The story of the Gautreaux litigation might make a book in itself. The plaintiffs' lawyers had to prove that the racial segregation of Chicago's housing projects was the result of intentional discrimination. They succeeded by uncovering evidence that white members of the Chicago City Council had an unofficial veto over the construction of public housing in their own wards. In 1968 Gautreaux, who had recently moved out of public housing, died of cancer at the age of forty-one. Her suit went on. The following year, federal judge Richard Austin, a friend of Mayor Richard J. Daley's who had not previously been considered an ally of liberal causes, ruled that the housing authority had broken the law. Under the terms of Judge Austin's order, the CHA was required to build three-quarters of its future units in white neighborhoods around the city.

When, in a seeming effort to comply, the CHA proposed sites around the city for new housing the following year, twenty-four thosand white Chicagoans wrote letters of protest. The CHA came up with a neat solution to the objections; it simply quit building public housing. Not until 1991 were Chicago's first new public housing units, a few hundred scattered, low-density town houses, ready for tenants.

It was a side street of the Gautreaux litigation that ultimately led to substantial progress. In his original 1969 ruling, Judge Austin had dismissed HUD as a defendant on the ground that it had merely provided money that was spent in a discriminatory manner by the CHA. But in 1971 the U.S. Court of Appeals reversed Austin's decision. It held that HUD knew it was paying for segregated housing in Chicago and thus shared legal responsibility for it. The proper remedy, the appeals court subsequently ruled, would be a metropolitan-wide plan for desegregated public housing, one encompassing suburban areas that had not been party to the suit. HUD appealed to the U.S. Supreme Court, which had recently decided that metropolitan-wide busing was an improper remedy for school segregation in *Milliken* v. *Bradley*. But in 1976 the Supreme Court upheld the lower court's verdict against HUD by an 8–0 vote.

While *Gautreaux* was working its way through the courts, the nation's attitude toward public housing underwent a dramatic shift. In 1972 Pruitt-Igoe, an enormous project in St. Louis, was declared uninhabitable and blown up. In 1974 Congress began to phase out its old "bricks-and-mortar" strategy and replace it with a new method of subsidizing housing through vouchers. Under the program, which was known as Section 8, qualifying families could move into already existing private housing. As in public projects, they would contribute 30 percent of their adjusted incomes toward the rent. Within certain guidelines, HUD would pay the rest.

Under a compromise with the *Gautreaux* lawyers, HUD agreed to provide Section 8 certificates to allow the Chicago plaintiffs to move into nonsegregated, subsidized housing. The Leadership Council for Metropolitan Open Communities, a fair-housing group that grew out of the King movement, was given the contract to administer the program. This meant selecting tenants as well as finding landlords in white neighborhoods who would agree to rent apartments to them. The Gautreaux program thus became not only an important avenue for desegregation in Chicago but also the largest residential "mobility" program anywhere in the country. In the past two decades, it has helped to relocate 7,000 black Chicago families to 115 surrounding suburbs.

PAM JACKSON IS grateful to Gautreaux for making her escape possible. "When Dorothy fought for this, it was the best thing she could have done. She opened the door for a lot of people," she says. Jackson was eligible for the Gautreaux program because she had grown up in Chicago public housing. Getting admitted, however, tested the limits of her capacities. The first step was to make telephone contact on registration day. Registrants used to sign up in person at the Leadership Council's office on State Street, but as word of the program spread, the lines got longer and finally grew unmanageable. Now, on a single day in January, the Leadership Council registers the first two thousand people who succeed in getting through on twenty-five constantly ringing phone lines. Such hurdles serve a purpose. By "creaming," as public policy types term it, the Leadership Council increases the odds that those who get in will be tenacious people like Pam Jackson and that the program as a whole will prove a success.

The phone lottery is a tragic and fantastic event; the volunteers who take calls frantically pull people aboard life rafts knowing there isn't room for everybody. According to the phone company, the number of people trying to get through is usually about 10,000. It went as high as 17,000 in 1993, a few months after a seven-year-old boy named Dantrell Davis, who lived in the Cabrini Green project on the North Side, was shot to death by a sniper as he walked to school with his mother. But even that number is just a fraction of the pool of people who potentially could benefit from Gautreaux. There are 50,000 families, 150,000 people, in Chicago Housing Authority buildings—wind tunnels of despair like Stateway Gardens and Robert Taylor Homes, where the murder rate is twenty-two times that of the city. The volunteers also know that a majority of those who get through on the phone will drop out of the program or fail to find an apartment.

"I always get on the waiting list, I never get through," Jackson says. "I said, I know I'm not going to get through. I called again and again. And I got through." She was invited to a briefing at the Leadership Council's office. There, along with twenty-five other single mothers, she was told she had five days to procure birth certificates for her daughter and herself and to get letters of recommendation from two friends and her landlord. She was also informed that she would have to find her own apartment and that it had to be in the suburbs, an area remote and unfamiliar to her. After that session, "I was kind of skeptical," she says. "I go downtown and get lost. I've never been to the Water Tower. But I got me a map. I found my way." Jackson went to her bedroom closet to find the map for me; it was a large foldout plan of greater Chicago, with the Gautreaux-eligible jurisdictions—those with less than 30 percent black population—highlighted in pink. Stored with the map were several other mementos of Jackson's search: the apartment listings from suburban newspapers and a folded sheet handed out by Delores Irvin, the inspiring Leadership Council staff member who directly administers the program. On the sheet were three slogans in block capitals:

YOU CAN IF YOU THINK YOU CAN.

YOU HAVE A RESPONSIBILITY TO
EDUCATE YOURSELF.

NEVER DEPRIVE ANYONE OF HOPE.

"I was frustrated many a night," Pam says. "But I kept that poem."

Her faith was necessary. Initially Jackson ran headlong into a wall of refusal. Though landlords can't legally discriminate on the basis of race, they aren't required to accept Section 8 tenants. Most haven't heard of the Gautreaux program and have no interest in renting to someone with an inner-city accent. One landlord in Glenview told Jackson that she sounded like a nice person, but he didn't want to take a chance on a program for minorities. A comment like that could be the basis for a lawsuit, but Pam preferred to move on. "A lot of people told me no," she says. "I said, 'Thank you for your time.' A lot of times I wanted to give up. I said, 'Don't give up, Pam.' You get frustrated, but you can't give up."

After five rejections Jackson reached her current landlord, Mike Dibrowa, on the phone. She explained her situation, and he offered to show her the apartment he had available. When she arrived, he told her she seemed very intelligent and that he was willing to rent to her. The rent was $575. She would have to contribute 30 percent of her adjusted monthly income, which came to a little over $200; HUD would pay the rest. "It's yours if you want it," he said. "I told him, I thank him for giving me a chance." Dibrowa further endeared himself to his tenant by braving the killing Chicago heat wave of 1995 to repair her air conditioner. "If I have a problem, he comes out. If I call him, he calls back," Jackson says. To a former resident of slums and public housing, these are minor miracles. "I get a chill just thinking how blessed I am."

Not everyone in the Gautreaux program is so rhapsodic. During a week spent visiting participants I met, among others, a woman named Emma Wesley in the township of Round Lake Beach, a more remote exurban community near the Wisconsin border. Wesley had been thrilled by the offer of an apartment in an attached two-bedroom town house near an artificial lake with ducks and geese. But so scarring were her experiences since moving that she wanted to return to a black neighborhood, though not in the city, at the first opportunity. Her thirteen-year-old son was stopped on the thinnest of pretexts by the local police. He had been beaten up by a gang of white boys. Few people had even been civil to her since her move. Neighbors were trying to evict her for playing loud music and hanging laundry outside. She said these charges were totally fictitious; she didn't even have a stereo. But less than a mile from Emma Wesley, I met Alice Jackson, who was thriving in a similar environment. Since moving from Altgeld Gardens, part of the complex where Dorothy Gautreaux lived, Jackson had gotten off welfare, found a job, been promoted, and moved to a second, better apartment. Her two teenage sons were doing well academically. She was making enough money from her job at a Speedway station that they no longer qualified for free lunches at their school.

As in almost any program, there are stories of success and stories of failure. But Gautreaux is inarguably a program that works—and works, miraculously, to ameliorate the most tragic and intractable social evil in American life: the condition of the black underclass. According to James Rosenbaum, a sociologist at Northwestern University who has studied the program for many years, the benefits usually are not felt immediately. Children in Gautreaux families often suffer a drop in grades after switching to tougher schools and moving to new, culturally disorienting environments. Black families feel isolated at first and often encounter hostility from white neighbors. Over time, however, they do vastly better on every measure that counts—employment, wages, welfare dependency, performance in school, and likelihood of attending college.

It is difficult to quantify these results because you can't really compare Gautreaux participants to other ghetto families. Though they share similar characteristics on paper, those who make it through the program demonstrate higher levels of intangible qualities like courage, open-mindedness, and competence. In order to try to figure out what the apparent success of the program really means, Rosenbaum compared Gautreaux families who moved to the mostly white suburbs with Gautreaux families moving to better but still mostly black neighborhoods within the city limits of Chicago. Today all Gautreaux families go to the suburbs, and they must find their own apartments. But through the 1980s the program was fortuitously set up as a controlled experiment. The Leadership Council found the landlords; tenants were assigned at random to either the suburbs or the city.

The contrast between the two groups is illuminating. Of those participants with jobs before and after their moves, both city and suburban movers experienced an average 20 percent boost in wages. But Rosenbaum found that 74 percent of suburban movers had a job after moving—a substantially higher share than among those who moved within the city. Part of the reason is obvious: there is more work in the suburbs, especially in the rapidly growing area northwest of Chicago where most Gautreaux participants go. But there is also the beneficial effect of a middle-class environment in which work is the norm. "Seeing neighbors work, Gautreaux adults reported that they felt that they too could have jobs, and they wanted to try," Rosenbaum writes in a 1995 article in the journal *Housing Policy Debate*. "Whatever prevented some people from being employed in the past—lack of skills or lack of motivation—was not irreversible, and many took jobs after moving to the suburbs."

The change in environment has an even more pronounced effect on educational performance. Less than 5 percent of the children of Gautreaux suburban families dropped out of school, as against 20 percent for the city group. Fifty-four percent of the suburbanites went on to attend college—as compared to 21 percent in the city. Fifty-four percent is an even more impressive number when compared to the tiny fraction of those who make it to college from housing projects in the ghetto. Among the suburban movers, young people who did not go on to college were far more likely to be employed, at jobs with higher wages and better benefits. In his most recent paper, Rosenbaum concludes: "The early experiences of low-income blacks do not prevent them from benefiting from suburban moves. Programs that help people escape areas of concentrated poverty can improve employment and educational opportunities."

Some of the greatest benefits of Gautreaux can't be quantified. Through the program, white suburbia makes contact with black Chicago and both learn a lesson in tolerance. Most of the participants I met told affecting stories about encountering bigotry that subsequently dissolved into friendship, or at least respect. They themselves had joined the program with prejudices against white people. Experience had taught them differently. Now they wanted to explain to others that their own stereotypes had been wrong. Gautreaux is also a powerful story about the black middle class reaching back to help those left behind. The three women who run the program—Delores Irvin, Mary Davis, and Carla Long Jordan—have all lived in public housing and raised children on their own. They overcame and, at the cost of considerable self-sacrifice, are helping others overcome. All three are role models in the best sense; they encourage others not just to break out of poverty but to reach back in turn. Pam Jackson spoke powerfully of remembering where she came from, and of helping to bring others out of the ghetto. "The people I left in the back, I will never forget them," she says. "I was one of those little project girls." She has been telling friends in the city to drop what she describes as their negative attitudes and join her in suburbia.

One of the fascinating aspects of Gautreaux is that it succeeds while violating most of the current received wisdom about what government can and can't do. It is a program with something to offend just about everybody's political sensibilities: a costly effort at social planning ordered by the federal courts and implemented over community objections. According to what we are supposed to have learned about government, such a bleeding-heart liberal endeavor should flop for a dozen reasons. Consider the most common objections to it, moving from left to right.

To those who deem themselves radicals, Gautreaux constitutes an affront to multiculturalism. Instead of racial pride, it promotes not only old-fashioned integration but assimilation. One such critic writing in the *Houston Post* in 1994 compared the program to "ethnic cleansing." More reasonably, J. R. Fuerst, who teaches at the Loyola University School of Social Work in Chicago, complained in an op-ed article in the *Chicago Tribune* that "There are real problems with relocating families far from their friends, acquaintances and familiar surroundings simply because social engineers want to place poor young single mothers in racially integrated surroundings as a model." From a left perspective, Gautreaux also erodes one of the foremost bases of black political power: the inner-city projects. The lawsuit halted construction of public housing in Chicago in 1966 and has diverted money away from rehabilitation.

To neoliberals or New Democrats who are inclined to look for market-oriented solutions, Gautreaux is not based around any idea of decentralization, privatization, or choice. For those eligible, the only choice is about whether to enter the program in the first place. If you get in, you move to the white suburbs, where you are forced to live surrounded by people who are different from yourself. Bureaucrats at HUD, the most backward-looking of the old agencies, supervise and pay the bills. In political terms, neoliberals might also point out that Gautreaux is a classic example of what got the Democratic Party into trouble: a race-conscious remedy that helps underclass blacks at the expense of middle-class whites. It can make no appeal to the group whose ongoing defection has reduced the Democrats to a minority party.

To communitarians, who derive their political ideas from a gauzy vision of old-time, small-town America, Gautreaux draws upon an expansive definition of rights to trespass on local values. In his book *The True and Only Heaven,* Christopher Lasch criticizes the idea of the program directly, attacking King for his "ill-conceived campaign for open housing in Chicago." By calling for residential integration, Lasch contends, King was "demanding the dissolution of white communities whose only crime, as far as anyone could see, was their sense of ethnic solidarity." Howard Husock, a housing expert at the John F. Kennedy School of Government at Harvard, has also written several articles attacking Gautreaux along these lines. In an article in the communitarian quarterly *The Responsive Community,* Husock writes that "Gatreaux" (as he misspells it throughout) "is meant to allow favored families to, in effect, leapfrog up the housing ladder, not by dint of thrift and effort but because of the twin qualifications of race and minimal income." This, Husock contends, denigrates middle-class values like hard work.

To "new paradigm" moderate conservatives, Gautreaux not only ignores but explicitly rejects the concept of empowerment. It doesn't use incentives or entrepreneurship to revitalize blighted areas. Rather, Gautreaux assists the most competent and ambitious people in moving out of the ghetto, thus leaving blighted neighborhoods worse off than they were before. It provides an escape hatch for those who might otherwise make an urban enterprise zone a viable idea.

To neoconservatives, such an ambitious scheme for social betterment is by definition an exercise in futility. A 1976 article in *The Public Interest* declared that the program would "surely be ineffective." Conceding its apparent success in the same journal years later, Nathan Glazer doubts that it can do much to diminish racial segregation nationally. "Its scale can never match the huge size of the inner-city black ghettoes," he writes in the fall 1995 issue. Members of the black lower class are too different from members of the white middle class to be successfully acculturated in neighborhoods where the latter live. "To expect this to work, to take this as a model, is to demand too much," he writes.

To traditional conservatives, Gautreaux is simply government intervention run amok. HUD's attempts to build on the Gautreaux model, James Bovard writes in the *American Spectator,* "now amount to a project to dictate where welfare recipients live in every county, city, and cranny across the nation." Not only is it social engineering, it's a waste of taxpayers' money. To make matters worse, Gautreaux is a program imposed over the wishes of the majority by an activist federal judiciary at the behest of liberal lawyers.

And there are other objections that don't fit neatly into any political ideology. Though it affords a good bargain in the long run by reducing the cost of programs like welfare, Medicaid, and food stamps, and by turning public charges into taxpayers, Gautreaux is fairly expensive in the short term. Administration and placement assistance run $1,500–$2,000 per family. Section 8 certificates cost an average of $6,000 a year (though most of the families that enter the program are public housing residents who receive the voucher in place of benefits that cost about the same amount). Gautreaux works best in secret. If white bungalow dwellers don't know that the black family moving onto their block is being put there by a federal program, they are less likely to object. Only when they sense a plan to empty the vertical ghettos and their attendant ills into the horizontal expanses of the suburbs are they minded to organize in opposition. For this reason, the staff of the Leadership Council has mixed feelings about even the highly favorable publicity the program has received.

My point is not that all of the contemporary nostrums about government are wrong. Many of them are valid rejoinders to old practices and habits of mind. In the abstract, choice is obviously preferable to no choice, markets to planning, cheap to expensive, democratic decision making to court imposition, openness to secrecy, and so on. But when such characterizations are elevated to the level of panaceas and precepts, a bit of skepticism is warranted. Blissfully unaware of the fact that it has no wings, the Gautreaux program soars. What makes it work is a combination of intelligence, creativity, high idealism, and the dedication of its staff. These are the indelible qualities of good government. In the real world, they are constantly at war with bureaucratic inertia, cynicism, and self-interest.

Unfortunately, it was the latter series of qualities that won out when it came to trying to expand upon the Gautreaux model. In 1991 Congress funded a national demonstration project based upon Gautreaux; the following year, HUD Secretary Jack Kemp named the program Moving to Opportunity. Clinton's appointee as HUD secretary, Henry Cisneros, was also an admirer of Gautreaux and a champion of MTO, which in late 1994 finally began on a small scale in five cities. MTO was based on the idea of residential mobility, but it was more contemporary in its design than Gautreaux: it would be based on class, not race; it would have a "study" component built in; there would be no court order; there would be no slyness.

The result was disaster. Before it even began, opposition to MTO exploded. In Baltimore, rumors spread that the city's black mayor, Kurt Schmoke, was going to tear down its public housing projects and disperse their eighteen thousand residents into white neighborhoods. In two working-class suburbs east of Baltimore, incendiary flyers began to circulate; angry meetings were held, and the *Sun* published editorials misrepresenting the program. A candidate running for the Baltimore County Council warned that the area would be flooded with people who would have "to be taught to take baths and not steal." Rather than defend the concept, liberals fled. The Clinton administration's effort to expand MTO was soon killed by one of its own, Democrat Barbara Mikulski, who at the time chaired the Senate subcommittee that oversees HUD. Mikulski described the program as too "controversial."

Today Gautreaux itself is on the way out, a victim of the Republican revolution. After twenty years, it has nearly reached the target of 7,100 families set by the consent decree. The success of the program makes a strong argument for continuation, but there appears to be no way for that to happen. HUD lawyers fought the court order for years and are not about to ask for its terms to be renewed. Though Cisneros admires the program, his attempt to build upon it failed. At the moment he is trying to slash enough from his department's budget to fend off conservative hotheads who want to eliminate it completely. There is no money. If Gautreaux closes down as expected in 1996, it will have gainsaid one last political verity: that no program ever comes to an end after having achieved its objective.

From Chicago I went to Washington, where Congress was in the midst of passing a drastic revision of a far vaster government effort: welfare. After a week spent with people who had actually escaped public assistance and some who were still struggling to do so, the debate had a surreal quality to it. Republican senators, one after another, took the floor to take credit for an effort to break the cycle of dependency, to move people from welfare to work, to resist illegitimacy. The women I met in Chicago had actually done this; their children were headed toward better lives, in better places. But they had made the change with massive help from the federal government. The Republican supporters of welfare reform insisted that they wanted others to follow the path these women had traveled, from dependency to self-reliance. But they were stepping back from the government's commitment to them. Under their plan, Washington would cease to be responsible. The next Pam Jackson would be on her own.

The bill that subsequently passed both houses is a sign of the times. Though it calls itself reform, it is really a retreat. Between 1935 and 1995, the federal government provided a minimal income of last resort to families with young children. Now even Democrats agree that Washington should make no guarantee. Under the new disposition, single mothers must find jobs. If they aren't capable of performing them, or there are none, tough luck. Welfare is a problem for the governors. In the Senate, only eleven Democrats voted against ending the federal welfare entitlement. The "reluctant" supporters of the Republican bill included such liberal stalwarts as Minority Leader Thomas Daschle and Christopher Dodd of Connecticut.

The welfare withdrawal is, of course, part of a much larger story. In a frenzy of unmaking, Congress is dumping government that works, government that doesn't, and a great deal that falls somewhere in between. In 1995 the stale metaphor that making legislation is like making sausage took on a new poignancy. Taxes were chopped, farm programs diced, Medicaid pureed. In a matter of a few days Medicare, one of the largest and most popular federal programs, was ground up and presented as a new, improved product to America's senior citizens. The pace of change was such that it was impossible for legislators, let alone concerned citizens, to truly understand all that was taking place. What happened in 1995 amounted to a kind of anti–New Deal, an alphabet soup of abolition instead of invention. The rapidity of the transformation has since slowed, and many specific changes have been blocked, but the direction is unlikely to change in the near future. Notions of "smaller" and "less" have captured not just the Republican cloakroom but the political imagination of the nation. Like conservatives in the New Deal era, liberals now function not as an engine in the opposite direction but as a brake on change.

In the chapters ahead, I examine the ongoing conservative assault on government and the most typical responses to it. It is my contention that while the conservative critique of government is incoherent and at times transparently dishonest, most of the replies liberals have offered are insufficient. Our government has serious flaws. It is overdrawn and overextended. It lacks accountability and flexibility. Its purposes have become muddied and often lost. The antigovernment moment we are now living through has been abetted by real failures.

To pretend otherwise only perpetuates the reaction against it. The true friends of government, as James Madison called them, have to do more than defend what is, and what we have done in the past. We need an activist government more than ever to heal the injuries of race and to reverse our growing stratification based on class. But if we aspire to use government for such ambitious purposes, we must first repair it. The loss of public faith is a complex phenomenon, but it is based on realities. Until we overthrow those realities, we cannot hope to win back the public's trust. And without that trust, we cannot act. What's needed is not a matter of what has come to be called "reinventing," making government more efficient and pragmatic. Doing so is a worthy objective, to be sure, but it plays into the illusion that we can avoid hard choices, that we can have more and better government at a lower cost. Government has a problem of ends as well as means. A fundamental reconsideration is now called for. In the final chapter, I try to lay out an alternative approach.

It is an unfortunate construct of language that we refer to government in the third person, as an *it.* That too easily makes it into an alien and oppressor, a leviathan, a monolithic and inhuman thing. In a liberal democracy like ours, the pronoun we should use is the first person plural. Government is *us,* collectively. The largeness and the power are our own. If government in this country acts the part of the oppressor or the tyrant, it is we who are oppressing ourselves. Government's flaws are our flaws, writ large, its failures our failures. But the successes of government are ours too—Pam Jackson's apartment, the preservation of the American wilderness, the rise of labor standards, the WPA, the Social Security system, the defeat of Hitler, integration, the landing on the moon, and the victory over communism. All were the products of an activist government, one with courage, confidence, and the nation's support. That kind of American government is presently dormant. What follows is an explanation of its decline and an argument about how to make it ours again.

Chapter One

THE REVOLT ⸱

It cannot have escaped those who have attended with candor to the arguments employed against the extensive powers of the government, that the authors of them have very little considered how far these powers were necessary means of attaining a necessary end. They have chosen rather to dwell on the inconveniences which must be unavoidably blended with all political advantages; and on the possible abuses which must be incident to every power or trust of which beneficial use can be made. This method of handling the subject cannot impose on the good sense of the people of America.

— JAMES MADISON, *The Federalist, No. 41,* 1788

REJECTION OF big government is the most powerful political sentiment in the land, and only the Republicans are responding to it," Congressman Dick Armey wrote in the Capitol Hill newspaper *Roll Call* in August 1994. At the time, his words attracted no attention whatsoever. The conventional wisdom had Republicans picking up a couple of dozen seats as a result of Bill Clinton's unpopularity, but certainly not winning control of both houses of Congress for the first time in forty years. Armey himself, a burly, voluble professor of economics from North Texas

State University, was hardly a figure to be reckoned with. Best known in the early part of his career for trying to save money by sleeping on a cot in the House gym, he continued to bear the disheveled look of someone who did. Among journalists covering Capitol Hill, Armey's antifederal fulminations were taken about as seriously as calls for the legalization of drugs or the reimposition of the gold standard. *The Almanac of American Politics* said he was "hardly likely to be a power in the House." Even his Republican colleagues tended to roll their eyes at his rants.

Everyone knows, of course, what happened three months later. The Republicans overran Capitol Hill after winning solid majorities in both the House and the Senate. Democrats lost control of committees theirs since 1954. Elevator operators under their patronage went looking for new work. The taxpayer-subsidized barbershop was shut down. Republicans were suddenly free to sleep wherever they pleased. Whole delegations flipped, such as that of the state of Washington, which went from 8–1 Democratic to 7–2 Republican. The defection of southern Democrats, a movement thought by some to have ended with Clinton's election in 1992, resumed with a vengeance.

The Clinton agenda, which consisted for the most part of creating new federal programs, became a dead letter overnight. Newt Gingrich's Contract with America took its place. It consisted of ten promises—to Republicans the new Ten Commandments. Armey was suddenly majority leader. Voting for him were seventy-three new Republican members, many of them political novices unknown beyond their own districts. One was a former homeless man from Texas, another a self-described former cocaine addict from Tennessee, another a semi-employed lawyer from Chicago who quadrupled his salary when he defeated Dan Rostenkowski, the powerful chairman of the Ways and Means Committee, who just a few years before was deemed invincible.

How had Democrats failed to see what was coming? It was apparent, at the very least, from polls. Asked in May 1994, "When the government in Washington decides to solve a problem, how much confidence do you have that the problem will be solved?" just 4 percent of respondents said, "a lot." Of the 64 percent who said "none at all" or "just a little," better than a 3–1 majority said the reason was that "government is incompetent," not that "those problems are often difficult to solve." On almost every question that the public opinion profession has devised to measure confidence in government, a similar disenchantment surfaces. Sixty-nine percent think the federal government creates more problems than it solves. Seventy percent agree that when something is run by the government, it is usually inefficient and wasteful. The same 70 percent are dissatisfied with "the overall performance of the national government of the United States." And so on.

The midterm election of 1994 was a period marker, indicating the end of the New Deal and the beginning of a new chapter in American politics. It not only changed the view of the future but also radically altered interpretation of the recent past. The new guiding principle was distaste for government. After the election, this dissatisfaction turned to truculence punctuated by bursts of absurdity. In Montgomery County, Maryland, for instance, a Democratic official announced his plan to drop the word *government* from official usage. It was, he said, "off-putting" and "arrogant."

In Congress, the tone was set by the Republican freshmen, a claque so ferociously antigovernment that they made Armey himself look like a thoughtful moderate. Stylistically, class members owed something to their least favorite decade, the 1960s. They had a strong taste for stunts and guerrilla theater, albeit with a narrower imaginative range. Radical chic was now a conservative phenomenon. When the Senate was deliberating the balanced budget amendment, the House freshmen marched across Capitol Hill in an attempt to put pressure on the upper chamber. In their private planning conclave, one member suggested that they bring live chickens to show their contempt for the Menshevik faction of their party.

The radicals of the new Congress took to the House floor to

deliver rant upon rant against "Washington," "the welfare state," and the world "inside the Beltway." Attacking "big government" and "bureaucrats" became for Republicans what "flower power" and "stop the war" had been twenty-five years earlier. On C-SPAN, fresh-faced apparatchiks like George Radanovich of California lamented that their districts paid more in taxes than they got back in federal spending—as if the government had no legitimate function at all, not even defending our borders. During the debate over term limits, an early defining episode, young Republicans scoffed at their elders with Lettermanesque sarcasm. Why was it so important to have experienced legislators? Mark Sanford from North Carolina wondered. "It's not like we're dealing with brain surgery," he sneered. At their worst (something they were at frequently), the new arrivals seemed like pod-people: cadres programmed for a mission to search and destroy. They made even the Reagan Robots, the freshmen elected in the Republican sweep of 1980, seem soft on liberalism.

The goal of these radicals was and remains, quite simply, the one Armey asserted: to strip the federal government of the functions it has taken on over the past ninety years. In some cases they argue for dispensing with responsibilities that have gone unquestioned since the early days of the Republic, such as the patent office and the postal system. If the Constitution proves an obstruction, they have few qualms about changing it. Some of the newcomers have signed on to as many as a half-dozen constitutional amendments, not just the conservative staples like banning abortion, allowing prayer in schools, and balancing the budget, but also more extreme ones, like requiring a supermajority for tax increases, letting states set their own term limits for federal officeholders, and removing First Amendment protection for flag burning.

At the feverish frontier of the elective right there has appeared a new breed of states'-rights zealot who truly sees the federal government as a malevolent force. Unlike the old southern variety of antifederalists concerned with preserving the traditional prerogatives of race, these are mostly westerners obsessed with federal efforts to regulate the private ownership of firearms and control the use of public lands. Steve Stockman of Texas has written that the attack on the Branch Davidian compound in Waco was part of a government conspiracy to justify gun control. Helen Chenoweth of Idaho, whose campaign was supported by her state's "militia" organization, sponsored a bill she called the Civil Rights Act of 1995; it would require federal authorities to obtain permission from local sheriffs before conducting searches or even carrying weapons. Her response to the Oklahoma City bombing was to assert that the country needed to "look at the public policies that may be pushing people too far."

To an alarming degree, such far-right paranoia has infected mainstream Republican politics. Before the bombing, in February 1995, Rush Limbaugh, perhaps America's most popular conservative, remarked, "The second violent American revolution is just about—I got my fingers about a fourth of an inch apart—is just about that far away. Because these people are sick and tired of a bunch of bureaucrats in Washington driving into town and telling them what they can and can't do." Such rhetoric used to be the province of southern populists defending segregation. Now even softhearted old moderates in the G.O.P. have glommed on to the antigovernment theme. "I think people feel government has grown too large, too centralized, too dictatorial," said William Roth, chairman of the Senate Finance Committee. Roth is mumbly and barely conscious in hearings, *mortis* without the *rigor*. For him to have caught the fever indicates the virulence of the virus. Another born-again zealot is Pete Wilson, the governor of California, notorious among conservatives for raising taxes early in his term. Announcing what proved to be a rather brief presidential candidacy, Wilson said: "California will not submit its destiny to faceless federal bureaucrats, or even congressional barons. We declare to Washington that California is a proud and sovereign state, not a colony of the federal government." A century or so earlier, such talk would have meant civil war.

Perhaps the most abrupt transformation was Bob Dole's. To true-blue conservatives, Dole is an infamous squish, one who has voted regularly not only for tax increases but for regulatory juggernauts like the Americans with Disabilities Act and the Civil Rights Act of 1990. Newt Gingrich once famously excoriated him as "the tax collector of the welfare state." After the 1994 election, however, Dole was like a tardy commuter chasing after a train as it pulls away from the station. As a presidential candidate, he has become a devotee of the Tenth Amendment, a copy of which he pulls from his pocket and reads at rallies: "The powers not delegated to the United States by the Constitution, nor prohibited by it to the states, are reserved to the states. . . ." His announcement speech developed this theme. "My mandate as president would be to rein in the federal government in order to set free the spirit of the American people," Dole told the crowd in his hometown of Russell, Kansas, in April 1995. "Reining in government, reining in government—it resonates with people out there," he told the *Washington Times*. Like George Bush before him, Dole has an amusing tendency to read not only his lines but the stage directions as well.

Dole's rival, Phil Gramm, meanwhile, needed no prompting. The 1994 election merely liberated him to sound as ferociously antigovernment as he really is. If most Republicans view taxation as excessive, Gramm goes them one better: he casts it as arbitrary confiscation. "We are one step away," he said in the announcement of his unsuccessful presidential candidacy, "from getting our money back." In another early campaign speech, Gramm compared Dole to Neville Chamberlain for having expressed willingness to work with the Clintons on health care reform. When Britain "decided to . . . stand up to the Nazis, they didn't turn to somebody who was yesterday for appeasement," he told an Iowa audience. In a bellicose mood, Ronald Reagan might discuss the commonalities between big government liberalism and communism. It took Gramm to liken Clinton to Hitler.

Such talk became muted for a time after April 21, when it became evident that the murder of 166 people in Oklahoma City was the work of antigovernment fanatics. The Republicans were caught in the awkward position of having loudly cursed a neighbor who suddenly drops dead. Those who casually blamed immorality on the influence of Hollywood were unwilling to concede their rhetoric might have encouraged the right's violent fringe, but they piped down. Examples of antigovernment hysteria were scarcer for a time, and intemperate remarks drew stiff criticism from Democrats and even from a few moderate Republicans. Still, the underlying sentiment remained the same. According to a May 1995 poll by the Gallup organization, 39 percent of respondents agreed that the federal government "has become so large and powerful it poses an immediate threat to the rights and freedoms of ordinary citizens." Within a few months of the bombing, the verbal aggression of the Republicans returned. By late summer, House Whip Tom DeLay, a former exterminator and antiregulatory fanatic, was back on the floor calling EPA officials "Gestapo."

The Antifederalist Society

Suspicion of concentrated government power is one of the great motifs of American political history. We fought our revolution against it. Independence, however, invited the opposite problem: a national government that was too weak to function effectively. In strengthening it, the framers of the Constitution strove to avoid creating a government that could become too strong; their primary preoccupation was the abuse of power, whether by an ambitious executive or a popular majority. The antifederalists who opposed the Constitution argued that extension of national authority would lead inextricably to abuse. Any power greater than that authorized by the Articles of Confederation would degenerate into monarchy, despotism, and tyranny. "What compensation then are you to receive in return for the liberties and privileges belonging to yourselves and posterity, that you are now about to sacrifice at the altar of this *monster,* this

Colossus of despotism?" asked the antifederalist writer "Philadelphiensis" in the *Freeman's Journal* in 1787.

In the heated Virginia ratifying convention of the following year, the leading statesmen expressed only slightly milder versions of this revulsion. One of the strongest opponents of "consolidation" was the revolutionary hero Patrick Henry. "If you make the citizens of this country agree to become the subjects of one great consolidated empire of America, your government will not have sufficient energy to keep them together. There will be no real checks, no real balances, in this government," he declaimed. George Mason, who had been a delegate to the Constitutional Convention but refused to sign the document, raised his own strong objection: "The very idea of converting what was formerly a confederation to a consolidated government is totally subversive of every principle which has hitherto governed us."

Mason struck a popular chord when he objected in particular to giving the federal government the power to lay taxes. In parts of the country, the prerevolutionary discontent with unrepresented taxation rapidly transformed itself into an objection to taxation per se. The most virulent expression of this sentiment was the Whiskey Rebellion, a violent revolt in the backcountry of Pennsylvania against a new federal excise tax. The slogan of the whiskey rebels might have been No New Taxes; they wanted to take back their country from out-of-touch, free-spending Washington bureaucrats. "Their detestation of the excise law is now universal, and has now associated to it a detestation of the government," Thomas Jefferson wrote Madison after receiving a report of the rebellion. The Alleghenies raged until President Washington and Treasury Secretary Alexander Hamilton appeared on the scene with fifteen thousand troops to quell the uprising.

In the early years of the Republic, Jefferson was the most eloquent critic of expanding federal power. Initially he was ambivalent about the powers given to the government by the framers, but after ratification of the Constitution, he became a strict constructionist. The federal government was fine so long as it remained limited to the powers enumerated in Article One. Jefferson consequently opposed Hamilton's sponsorship of the First Bank of the United States. "To take a single step beyond the boundaries thus specially drawn around the powers of Congress is to take possession of a boundless field of power, no longer susceptible of any definition," he wrote in 1791.

The Sedition Act of 1798 substantiated Jefferson's fears. Created to deal with conspiracies against the government, it made defamation of Congress or the president a crime. With requisite hyperbole, Jeffersonian Republicans called the latter years of the John Adams administration the "Federalist Reign of Terror." Jefferson himself ghost-wrote the set of resolutions that the Kentucky state legislature passed to indicate its displeasure with the law. He argued strenuously that the Sedition Act was unconstitutional, even going so far as to assert that states were not legally bound by it. Madison made a similar argument as the unnamed author of the Virginia Resolutions. These claims were never tested; the issue of whether states could declare a federal law unconstitutional was made moot by the expiration of the Sedition Act in 1800 and by Jefferson's election to the presidency the same year. But after Chief Justice Marshall arrogated for the Supreme Court the right to decide what was and wasn't constitutional, in *Marbury* v. *Madison,* Jefferson became worried about the growing power of the judiciary. He later called the Supreme Court a "corps of sappers and miners, steadily working to undermine the independent rights of the states, and to consolidate all power in the hands of the government."

Jefferson's concerns were many. He feared the moral hazards of a large bureaucracy and a well-funded treasury. "What an augmentation of the field for jobbing, speculating, plundering, office-building and office-hunting would be produced by an assumption of all the state powers into the hand of the general government!" Jefferson wrote to his political ally Gideon Granger in 1800. "The true theory of our Constitution is surely the wisest and best, that the states are independent as to everything within themselves and united as to everything respecting foreign nations. Let the general government be reduced to foreign concerns only." One of Jefferson's first acts as president in 1801 was to repeal the national estate and property taxes that had been imposed a few years earlier. Limited government, he theorized, could easily be undermined by bountiful resources.

By his actions as president, however, Jefferson recognized that there were demands on government that the minimalist state could not easily handle, and so the federal government grew. In 1803 he doubled the size of the United States with the Louisiana Purchase. But the Jeffersonian persuasion continued to serve groups and classes of people who feared government for a wide variety of reasons. In the Jacksonian era, the high-minded, strict constructionist view of the Constitution was taken up by southern planters whose livelihood was threatened by federal tariffs on imported goods. "Who are the true friends of the Union?" Robert Hayne of South Carolina asked in an 1830 Senate speech. "Those who would confine the Federal government strictly within the limits prescribed by the Constitution," he answered, "who would preserve to the states and the people all powers not expressly delegated; who would make this a federal and not a national union." John C. Calhoun, then vice president to Andrew Jackson, espoused the doctrine of "nullification." This was a revival of the notion Jefferson and Madison had flirted with in the controversy over the Alien and Sedition Acts in 1798: states could refuse to allow the enforcement of laws they deemed unconstitutional. South Carolina, which led the revolt, backed down only under Jackson's threat to use federal force.

But Jackson himself fretted over the expanding functions of the federal government. In 1830 he vetoed a bill passed by Congress to build the Maysville road in Kentucky. Jackson's theory was that federal sponsorship of "internal improvements" of local rather than national import were not permitted by the Constitution. (Henry Clay, who represented Kentucky in the Senate, pointed out that Jackson had supported other such projects when it suited his own political purposes.) One finds the Jeffersonian view of the Constitution again in Jackson's 1832 veto of the recharter of the Bank of the United States. Jackson thought the central bank had created opportunity for those with the greatest economic power to take advantage of the federal government. "It is to be regretted," he thundered in his veto message, "that the rich and powerful too often bend the acts of government to their selfish purposes."

The Democratic platform of 1840, the first such national party document, begins with the words: *"Resolved,* That the federal government is one of limited powers. . . ." The rest of the brief statement delineates what government can't do: carry out internal improvements, assume the debts of states, charter a national bank, or interfere with slavery. In 1860 the Republicans, in their own first platform, sounded a similar note: *"Resolved* . . . That the people justly view with alarm the reckless extravagance which pervades every department of the Federal Government; that a turn to rigid economy and accountability is indispensable to arrest the systematic plunder of the public treasury by favored partisans."

Though the post–Civil War amendments to the Constitution put an end to the most expansive view of states' rights, they did not squelch objections to the growth of Washington's authority. Democrats objected that the martial powers adopted by President Lincoln during the war were inimical to the Constitution. Radicals of Lincoln's own party argued that his pocket veto of the Wade-Davis bill, which prescribed harsh terms for southern readmission to the union, was an act of executive tyranny. Though the size and the cost of government grew with the expansion of veterans' pensions and widows' benefits after the war, neither party wished to claim the mantle of big government. Each divvied up spoils and sinecures among its partisans when in power. And each, when out of power, accused the other of usurping local responsibilities, overspending, and plundering the Treasury for the sake of patronage.

Cynicism about government was never more prevalent, and never more justified, than during the last three decades of the nineteenth century. American politics was more corrupt than ever before. Bribery was practiced with guiltless impunity; one congressman in 1873 described the House of Representatives as an auction room "where more valuable considerations were disposed of under the speaker's hammer than in any other place on earth." After Benjamin Harrison was elected president in 1888, he was appalled to discover that he could not even choose his own cabinet, since Republican Party leaders had already sold off all of the best positions to get him elected. These spoilsmen of the Gilded Age spawned a genre of antigovernment humor we still endure today. "It could probably be shown by facts and figures that there is no distinctly native American criminal class except Congress," Mark Twain remarked in *Following the Equator* (1897). Modifying Twain's crack, Ambrose Bierce defined politics in his *Devil's Dictionary* (1906) as "a means of livelihood affected by the more degraded portion of our criminal class."

After the reforms of the Progressive era cleared away the most blatant forms of corruption, popular suspicion of politicians assumed milder forms. The antigovernment jokes of the 1920s were, by comparison to previous decades, gentle, even affectionate. Politicians weren't corrupt, they were just a bit wacky. Thus most of the humor of Will Rogers, and Irwin S. Cobb's remark, "If I wanted to go crazy I would do it in Washington because it would not be noticed." To the extent the parties differed in their conceptions of government, the roles to which we are now accustomed were reversed. Republicans, who controlled the presidency for fifty-six of the seventy-two years between 1860 and 1932, were by virtue of winning elections the party of the federal government. Democrats were the party of states' rights. The fairly characteristic Democratic platform of 1924 condemned the G.O.P for its "centralizing and destructive tendencies" and denounced the Coolidge administration for its "extension of bureaucracy." Even Franklin D. Roosevelt worked this vein, complaining in the 1932 campaign about Herbert Hoover's irresponsible failure to balance the federal budget.

This situation was permanently reversed with the New Deal. Conservatives depicted Roosevelt's program not just as an unconstitutional usurpation of power but as an incipient totalitarian dictatorship. To Hoover, writing in his 1934 jeremiad *The Challenge to Liberty,* it was "the most stupendous invasion of the whole spirit of Liberty that the nation has witnessed since the days of Colonial America." Fear of expanding federal power was not confined to those the president called "economic royalists." As Alan Brinkley points out in his book *Voices of Protest,* the populists Father Coughlin and Huey Long railed against the growth of government through the Depression years, their attacks on big business and calls for the redistribution of wealth notwithstanding. "The very nature of its development makes inroads upon the rights of citizens; its ultimate goal is inevitably some type of tyranny," Coughlin said. Long described the new alphabet agencies as "contrary to the American system."

Throughout the Roosevelt-Truman years, Republicans maintained their position as opponents of expansive government. The Taft-Goldwater tradition in Republican politics was built around the call for repealing New Deal social programs like Social Security. "I fear Washington and centralized government more than I do Moscow," Goldwater said in 1960. Antigovernment Republicanism was, however, a largely inert force through most of the Cold War era; successful politicians tended to be those who recognized the consensus surrounding the New Deal welfare state.

Deep antifederalist feeling did not return until the 1960s, when white southerners reached for a principle to assert against racial integration. In the person of George Wallace, the arguments of Hayne and Calhoun were reborn. In 1963 Wallace explained his attempt to block integration of the University of Alabama: "When I go to stand in the door, it is to raise dramatically the question of sovereignty of the state. It is raising a constitutional question. . . . Does the state of Alabama run its school system, or does the federal court and the Justice Department?" Appearing on *Meet the Press* a few days later, Wallace said of his obstructionism: "I think it is a dramatic way to impress upon the

American people this omnipotent march of centralized government that is going to destroy the rights and freedom and liberty of the people of this country if it continues, and we in Alabama intend to resist this centralized control, where they now tell us whom you can eat with and whom you can sit down with and swim with and whom you can sell your house to."

Another old theme reemerged in the following decade: resistance to government's use of its taxing power. This upsurge commanded national attention as a result of Proposition 13, the California property tax limitation ballot initiative of 1978. But the movement was soon nationalized with the presidential campaign and victory of California's former governor Ronald Reagan. "Government is not the solution, it's the problem," Reagan famously declared in his 1981 inaugural address, putting the proposition in the most elemental terms possible. This notion was a staple of Reagan's public utterances, which ranged from his famous promise in his 1980 debate with Jimmy Carter "to take government off the backs of the great people of this country," to one of his favorite jokes, "the nearest thing to eternal life we'll ever see is a government program," and his oft-repeated crack that the ten most frightening words in the English language are: "Hello, I'm from the government, and I'm here to help."

Reagan located big-government liberalism on a continuum with totalitarian communism. "For some decades now, the liberal movement has worked to centralize government authority in Washington and to increase government's power. . . . We find the ultimate in government planning in the Soviet Union," he wrote before his election. "Runaway government threatens our economic survival, our most cherished institutions, and the very preservation of freedom itself," he said in 1982. In another speech Reagan described "government careening out of control, pushing us toward economic collapse, and quite probably the end of our way of life."

Revenge of the Gutless Herd

For all his brave talk, Reagan flinched when it came to confronting directly the size and scope of the federal government. His hyperbolic rhetoric camouflaged this reality, so much so that many liberals never realized that the "Reagan budget cuts" were mostly a figment of their own propaganda. "Despite the caterwauling about Reagan's supposedly savage budget cuts in 1981, not one major spending program was abolished during the Reagan presidency," writes the conservative critic David Frum in *Dead Right.* "Only one spending program of any size was done away with, and even that—the Comprehensive Employment and Training Act—was instantly replaced by another program, the Jobs Partnership Training Act, meant to achieve almost exactly the same end." In fact, federal spending, figured as a share of Gross Domestic Product, grew from 20.7 percent in 1979 to 23.3 percent in 1992. But receipts rose more slowly than expenditures, resulting in the structural budget deficit we have lived with ever since, and of our $5 trillion national debt.

After he left the administration, Reagan's budget director, David Stockman, became a voluble critic of the Republican failure to take on the welfare state. In his book *The Triumph of Politics: Why the Reagan Revolution Failed,* Stockman portrayed Reagan as childlike in his incomprehension of the situation his administration faced. Reagan wanted to shrink the government but was outraged at the suggestion that people might bleed as a result. He thought the necessary downsizing could be accomplished by ferreting out waste and abuse, something he believed he had done as governor of California. (In reality he raised taxes and increased spending at a rate of 12 percent a year.) Reagan remained impervious to all efforts to dispel his illusions. An even greater object of Stockman's scorn was what he called the "gutless herd of self-proclaimed conservative politicians." It was this group, he argued, that doomed the effort to reverse the growth of the welfare state. These legislators had their noses too deep in the congressional

pork barrel to remember their supposed disdain for big government. From his experience, Stockman concluded not just that the
Reagan revolution had failed but that the project of shrinking the
welfare state was once and forever an impossibility. Republicans
simply weren't serious about it.

This analysis looked more trenchant than ever during the
Bush years. For Reagan's successor, the attack on government
was clearly just talk. Bush's natural tendency was governmental.
He cooperated with Democrats in drafting new laws for environmental protection and civil rights; he boasted of spending
increases on education, crime, and drugs. The last straw for
many conservatives was when Bush broke a clear promise and
agreed to a major tax increase in 1990. In his book, published in
1994, Frum drew from the Bush experience an even more pessimistic version of Stockman's lesson. Handouts were what made
politicians popular. And Republican politicians, he argued, were
too addicted to being popular to take their own ideas seriously.

Things did indeed appear bleak for the advocates of limited government during the Bush years. But Stockman and Frum were both
excessively pessimistic—from their own point of view—in taking
phoniness about slimming government to be the eternal purgatory
of Republican politics. Partly in reaction to the Reagan-Bush failure, the antigovernment mood surged again, more powerfully
than before. One could read it in the sort of political book published
in the early nineties: *The Government Racket: Washington Waste from
A–Z,* by Martin L. Gross ("The government in Washington is out
of control—fiscally, morally, and philosophically.... Virtually
everything Washington does lacks both intellect and practical-
ity"); *Adventures in Porkland: How Washington Wastes Your Money
and Why They Won't Stop,* by Brian Kelly ("It's outrageous. It *has* to
stop. This isn't free money, we know that. The guys who are giving us back our own money and making us thankful for it are con
men who need to be tossed onto the street"); and *Club Fed,* by Bill
Thomas ("They *are* working together, working to keep their
privileges, money, and power as long as they can"). All rather wit-
less, but they testify to a national mood.

Antigovernment feeling, in various mutations, animated Ross Perot and the other "outsider" candidates of 1992. Bush's apostasy on the tax issue provoked Pat Buchanan to challenge him for the Republican nomination. Paul Tsongas and Jerry Brown ran for the Democratic nomination on themes of deficit reduction and political reform. Bill Clinton defeated them in the primaries by co-opting much of thier rhetoric, promising "a government that works better and costs less." In so doing, Clinton also echoed Perot, who promised to stop the government from squandering money, to make it function more like a business, and to prevent profiteers from taking corrupt advantage of it.

To be sure, the mood was less than distinct in 1992. Voters were "angry," but it was less than clear what they were angry about: taxes, spending, their standard of living, crime, immigrants, a changing country, modern life—the expression was an inchoate roar. It was possible, for instance, to read Perot's rhetoric as a demand either for smaller government and lower taxes or for sharper and more pragmatic intervention on issues like declining wages. The 1991 recession created a groundswell of support for federal involvement on a range of issues, including unemployment, the decline of the public infrastructure, and health care, that contradicted the notion of a backlash against government.

This ambiguity allowed Clinton to fudge the issue. To the so-called New Democrats, he embodied the notion of a smaller and more efficient government, one that would rely more on private-sector solutions, reform the welfare system, and attack the deficit. To old Democrats, on the other hand, he represented a promise to deliver the largest missing piece of the New Deal welfare state, universal medical coverage, to expand other programs, and to reverse Reaganomics. It all blurred under the rubric of "change." After his election, Clinton was far more interested in creating new programs than in dismantling old ones. He handed off the task of downsizing and rationalizing bureaucracies to Vice President Al Gore, while focusing his own energies on devising the newest government benefit.

To propose such a costly, complicated new program as univer-

sal health insurance in the midst of a rebellion against government now appears an act of gross political negligence, a pointless
escalation in a losing battle. But if Clinton was blind to the mood
of reaction against government, Republicans were slow to recognize its dimensions as well. The original response of the party's
congressional leadership to Clinton's health care initiative was
that it would work with the White House to answer a crying
need. The Republican political goal, at first, was simply to prevent Democrats from reaping all the credit for reform. To argue
against any intervention was considered a futile, extremist position. Former defense secretary Richard Cheney, who in early
1994 contemplated a presidential bid, was mocked by conservative strategists for his poor judgment in suggesting there was no
crisis sufficient to warrant federal action. It was only after the
Clinton-Rodham-Magaziner plan failed, its demise spurred by
an aggressive insurance industry propaganda effort, that Republicans began to take a more ideological stance against it. Not until
after the 1994 election did they realize it had been a central factor
in their victory.

After the election Clinton tried to convince everyone that he
had been the one cutting government all along. "We have already
eliminated or reduced three hundred programs," he boasted to
Newsweek. Vice President Gore was given center stage for a new,
reinvented "reinventing government" effort. Having figured out
how to make government bureaus run better, Gore was now
assigned to figure out how to get rid of them entirely. But if this
barn-door closing was a bit belated, even less persuasive was
Clinton's original 1996 budget proposal, which dropped the cause
of deficit reduction altogether. Though big government was
unpopular, Clinton reckoned shrinking it would be more unpopular still. He thought his own deficit reduction plan was what
had sent him so low in the polls. On this logic, he decided to hang
back and let the Republicans attack the deficit on their own.

Republicans had talked endlessly about cutting spending in
the past but had never really done it. So, in early 1995, there was at
least a plausible political argument for calling their bluff. But by

assuming Republicans weren't serious, Clinton made a strategic error: he was refighting the previous war. This time it was different; the Republicans meant business, a point Clinton subsequently acknowledged by proposing a second 1996 budget with more significant cuts. Conservatives were no longer content to leave their assault on government at the level of rhetoric. John Kasich, the new chairman of the House Budget Committee, made his point plainly after the election. If Republicans did not fulfill their promise to balance the budget, Americans would turn to a third party, he said, and be justified in doing so. In May, Kasich and his Senate counterpart, Pete Domenici, delivered budgets that did what had long been thought impossible. They spelled out specific cutbacks that would balance the budget by the year 2002. The House version cut enough to pay for several hundred billion dollars in tax cuts as well. The Republicans proposed a 30 percent reduction in domestic discretionary spending. In the fall, both houses passed an actual budget embodying these principles.

But it wasn't just a matter of budget balancing. In 1995 Republicans moved to give meaning to their old platitudes about federal power and states' rights. By turning established programs into block grants, they were attempting to alter fundamentally Washington's role in American life. It wasn't just a more modest version of the New Deal they were after. It was a return to the Jeffersonian conception of federalism, or at least a free-lunch Jeffersonianism in which Washington raises money and governors get to spend it.

After decades of posturing, conservatives were no longer just mouthing off against the federal government. They were trying to take it down. In the words of one impatient freshman, the time had finally come to "just do it." Today it is no longer possible to answer the Republican charge by pointing out that there isn't any cavalry. The barbarians are inside the gates. The assault is a reality.

Chapter Two

THE FALL OF PUBLIC TRUST

The central conservative truth is that it is culture, not politics, that determines the success of a society. The central liberal truth is that politics can change a culture and save it from itself.
— DANIEL PATRICK MOYNIHAN,
Family and Nation, 1986

THOUGH WE may not fully understand why the American public has lost faith in its government, we do know, by and large, when it happened. The drop-off follows a distinct course. The use of public opinion polls began early in FDR's second term. For almost three decades thereafter, national confidence grew along with the size and power of federal institutions. This era of good feelings continued until the mid-1960s, at which point it ended abruptly. Since then, polls have shown a consistent, growing dislike of government at all levels.

Since the 1940s, pollsters have asked: "How much of the time do you think you can trust the government in Washington to do what is right?" In 1964 some 76 percent answered "most of the time" or "always." Over the subsequent three decades, the slope of the positive response line has descended, over a few hills and valleys, nearly to sea level. In 1994, as Clinton was trying to pass his health care reform plan, it bottomed out at 14 percent. One

1995 survey had it back up at 18 percent, but that may not mean any more than past indications of resurgent confidence, which have all proven to be false cues.

The beginning of the decline corresponds to the stirrings of 1960s radicalism at Berkeley, the urban unrest that culminated in the Watts riot, and the initial protests against the Vietnam War. The most momentous drop, according to a thirty-year study by the University of Michigan Survey Research Institute, took place between 1965 and 1972. But the downward trend continued through the seventies and into the eighties. At the end of Reagan's first term, social scientists got excited about signs that public confidence was rising again. But the gains ebbed away as the Iran-contra scandal unfolded. Another boost connected to the success of the Gulf War petered out even more quickly.

How did America's faith in its government fall so far so fast? Broadly speaking, there are two competing explanations, a conservative and a liberal one. The conservative answer is that the decline is a *rational* response to the observed phenomenon of failure. The liberal explanation is that mass disillusionment with government is an *irrational* reaction, fueled by prejudice, fear, and economic insecurity. Let's consider the right's argument first.

The Conservative Version

Conservatives contend that government made a sudden wrong turn in the mid-1960s, with Lyndon Johnson's Great Society. Bigger government was no problem when it meant Franklin Roosevelt's New Deal, most of them hold. But under LBJ, public expansion took the shape of a heedless experiment in social engineering.

This is the view of the Republicans' two most important late-twentieth-century leaders: Ronald Reagan and Newt Gingrich. In his postpresidential autobiography, Reagan quotes a 1982 entry in his diary: "The press is trying to paint me as now trying to undo the New Deal. I remind them that I voted for FDR four times. I'm trying to undo the 'Great Society.' It was LBJ's war on poverty that led us to our present mess." As early as his first, unsuccessful campaign for Congress in 1974, Gingrich articulated the same distinction. One of his slogans was "Keep the New Deal but dismantle the Great Society." As Speaker of the House, Gingrich has called Roosevelt "the greatest president of the twentieth century." In his so-called coronation speech in January 1995, he asserted that he and his Republican colleagues would have voted for much of the New Deal had they been around at the time. In a conscious tribute, he styled his legislative push for the Contract with America on FDR's first hundred days.

By contrast, Gingrich and other Republicans have nothing but scorn for Johnson's legacy. "How are future generations likely to remember the Great Society?" Dick Armey wondered in an April 1995 op-ed piece. "As an explosion of well-intentioned but misguided government action that made poverty worse, broke up families, devastated inner cities, and led to a hemorrhage of red ink." Armey blames the Great Society not only for doubling the rate of teenage pregnancy but for a rise in teen suicides, a tripling of the crime rate, and a massive increase in divorce. His argument, echoed by countless other conservatives, is that Johnson's efforts to help the poor represented a departure from the old principles of self-help, initiative, and individual responsibility; Armey calls the Great Society a philosophy of "mandated charity" that "misdiagnosed poverty as a material rather than a moral phenomenon." In Gingrich's formulation, the Great Society "corrupted" and "ruined the poor."

The Armey-Gingrich argument evolves from one originally made by neoconservatives, the influential cluster of former liberal and socialist intellectuals who began to question their old beliefs and allegiances in the early 1970s. Disenchantment with domestic policy is not the most familiar aspect of neoconservatism; to Norman Podhoretz and the *Commentary* crowd, it was the New Left's soft spot for third-world socialism and its cultural radicalism that prompted a reconsideration and shift rightward. But while sharing those concerns, Irving Kristol and the more

academic group clustered around *The Public Interest* were motivated by an additional one: what they increasingly took to be the
failure of liberal social programs. The domestic neocons believed
in the New Deal, but they felt something had gone drastically
wrong during the Johnson years.

The first to develop this thesis in a serious way was Aaron
Wildavsky, a UCLA political scientist and member of the *Public
Interest* editorial board. Wildavsky's initial disenchantment grew
out of his study of a program sponsored by the Economic Development Administration in Oakland. The EDA was one of the
offices set up by the War on Poverty, and the Oakland Project,
which began in 1967, was one of its most highly touted efforts. Its
grandiose goal was to save Oakland from the violence that was
engulfing other cities by creating jobs for blacks. In the end, however, the project brought only a handful of jobs to Oakland at a
cost of several million dollars. *Implementation,* the book Wildavsky wrote with Jeffrey Pressman about the experience, tells
the story in its subtitle: *How Great Expectations in Washington Are
Dashed in Oakland; Or, Why It's Amazing That Federal Programs
Work at All, This Being the Saga of the Economic Development
Administration as Told by Two Sympathetic Observers Who Seek to
Build Morals on a Foundation of Ruined Hopes.*

Implementation is a scholarly account and as such rather tenta-
tive in its conclusions. But in 1973, the same year it came out,
Wildavsky drew upon his study for an article in *Commentary,*
"Government and the People." Here he did not hestitate to
extrapolate. There was a fundamental difference between the
New Deal and the Great Society models of intervention. The former, he asserted, was directed at a mass public suffering temporary
hardship, while the latter was focused on a much smaller, profoundly marginalized segment of society. "No previous government had ever attempted to do for this sector of the
population—those whom Marx had called the lumpenprole-
tariat—what the American government set out to do," Wildavsky wrote. "Nobody knew *how* to go about it, either."

This theme—that government was in over its head, trying to

solve problems it didn't even understand—was taken up by others: Kristol, Nathan Glazer, Daniel Patrick Moynihan, and James Q. Wilson. But the context of the early neoconservative critique was still support for big-government liberalism. Neoconservatives remained well disposed toward the "welfare state," which in the 1970s was still a neutral social-science term for the government wrought by the New Deal and the mixed economies of Western Europe. "Neoconservatism is not at all hostile to the idea of the welfare state, but it is critical of the Great Society version of the welfare state," Kristol wrote in a *Newsweek* essay in 1976. "In general, it approves of those social reforms that, while providing needed security and comfort to the individual in our dynamic, urbanized society, do so with a minimum of bureaucratic intrusion in the individual's affairs." Kristol's version of the argument was that the Great Society had gone wrong by removing the moral dimension from Roosevelt's edifice.

Kristol's ideas soon cross-pollinated with an older strain of conservatism that was indeed hostile not just to the Great Society but to the welfare state per se. The children of this marriage were David Stockman and Charles Murray, influential thinkers on the right during the 1980s. Stockman had studied with Glazer and Wilson as a divinity student at Harvard, and had worked for Moynihan as a baby-sitter. As he recalled in his book, he was strongly influenced by these teachers after he abandoned his youthful flirtation with Marxism and was gravitating toward the libertarianism of F. A. Hayek, Milton Friedman, and Barry Goldwater. For Stockman, the neoconservatives provided an evidentiary basis for conservative beliefs. It didn't matter whether government programs were justified in the abstract, because they didn't do any good anyhow.

As Stockman was attempting, with limited success, to pare back the programs that composed the welfare state, Murray was pushing a critique of liberal social policy still farther. In *Losing Ground* (1984) he made an even bolder case that government intervention on behalf of the poor wasn't just wasteful, inefficient, or oversold; it was actually counterproductive, making the very problems it attempted to solve worse than they would have been had the government done nothing at all. Following Kristol, Murray argued that the fundamental flaw in the War on Poverty was its absence of moralism; Johnson's programs fostered a no-fault attitude that had the effect of rewarding failure. "We tried to provide more for the poor and produced more poor instead," Murray wrote. "We tried to remove the barriers to escape from poverty, and inadvertently built a trap."

As the economist Albert O. Hirschman notes, this was a version of a very old rhetorical formulation, one he calls the "perversity thesis": any attempt to change society or ameliorate its problems will inevitably produce results opposite from those intended. In early-nineteenth-century Britain, critics of the Poor Laws argued that relief created an incentive to sloth, thereby increasing poverty instead of diminishing it. Then, as now, this was a deeply attractive formulation for conservatives, because it permitted them to attack progressive policies without seeming heartless. Indeed, it allows them to claim the banner of compassion as their own. As Murray understood, the perversity thesis is the ultimate trump card in political argument, because if its empirical basis is sound, there can be no response to it.

At the end of this evolution lies Gingrich, who owes his greatest intellectual debt to Murray. But given Murray's political radioactivity after the publication of *The Bell Curve,* Gingrich has tended to rely more upon Murray's disciples. Foremost among them is Marvin Olasky, a professor at the University of Texas and editor of the Christian magazine *World.* Gingrich constantly refers his listeners to Olasky's *The Tragedy of American Compassion,* to which Murray wrote the preface. In it Olasky argues that the New Deal was sound because it maintained the traditional distinction between the deserving and undeserving poor. The Great Society, by contrast, "helped sever welfare from shame in the minds of many dole-holders." Gingrich is also prone to cite Myron Magnet, editor of the neoconservative Manhattan Institute's magazine *City Journal* and another Murray disciple. Magnet's book *Dream and the Nightmare: The Sixties' Legacy to the*

Underclass elaborates upon *Losing Ground* with an argument that attitudinal changes—moral relativism and defining the poor as victims—laid the ground for the Great Society's failure. Magnet offers a trickle-down theory of deviancy: the amorality of white baby boomers legitimated self-destructive behavior on the part of lower-class blacks.

What Gingrich has done is take these arguments and shake them into a cocktail. In his implicit syllogism, the Great Society was the fruit of flawed moral attitudes of the 1960s; government failure is the product of the Great Society; ergo, bad government is the spawn of "the sixties." Taking this a step further, liberals (who supported the Great Society) are culpable for all manner of outrages. Hence, in Gingrich's view, Democrats bear responsibility for horrific crimes committed by members of the underclass as well as the actions of Susan Smith, who murdered her two sons and blamed it on a black car-jacker. They also deserve blame for Woody Allen, who left his common-law wife for her adoptive daughter. These far-flung connections begin to make sense when you understand that Gingrich views Woodstock as a Great Society program. In rebuffing the government of the Great Society, he asserts that the public rejects not just failure but immorality.

The Liberal Version

Liberals have an alternative story about what happened to faith in government—or at least about what happened to faith in them, which amounts to more or less the same thing. They believe their party lost its majority status over the issue of race.

Their argument goes something like this: Before 1964 Republicans were more closely associated with a liberal view of civil rights. Theirs was the northern-dominated party of Lincoln; Democrats were still the party of the white South and Jim Crow. Though presidents Roosevelt, Truman, and Kennedy took significant steps on behalf of blacks, none faced the issue squarely until Johnson dedicated himself to passing the Civil Rights Act of

1964. In so doing, LBJ launched his party on a righteous path, but one that unfortunately led to a political wilderness. As Democrats became the party of racial change, Republicans sensed a political void and opportunistically filled it by becoming the party of racial reaction. The 1960 Republican platform had a strong civil rights plank. The party's 1964 platform, by contrast, had no civil rights plank. Its nominee, Barry Goldwater, campaigned against desegregation and opposed the Civil Rights Act. When the segregationist Democrat George Wallace withdrew as a third-party candidate in that year's campaign, it was to Goldwater not Johnson that he threw his support.

The congressional divide on the Voting Rights Act of 1965 ratified the new pattern; Democrats supported it by a far greater margin than Republicans. From then on, the G.O.P was entrenched as the party that opposed federal intervention on the race question. This switch induced Republican gains in the 1966 midterm election, and Richard Nixon's victory over Hubert Humphrey in 1968. Fifty-seven percent of the electorate voted either for Nixon or for Wallace that year. In the presidential election of 1972, the South went overwhelmingly Republican for the first time.

Ironically, it was a Republican strategist, Kevin Phillips, who first formulated what subsequently became a liberal catechism: Republicans obtained majority status by wooing disaffected whites. A Nixon campaign aide working under John Mitchell in 1968, Phillips was the first to apply the idea of realignment as a Republican strategy. After the election, he published *The Emerging Republican Majority,* originally a Nixon campaign document, that pointed to race as a lever by which the G.O.P could pry votes away from the Democrats, particularly in the South.

The principal prevailing force which broke up the Democratic (New Deal) coalition is the Negro socioeconomic revolution and the liberal inability to cope with it. Democratic "Great Society" programs aligned that party with many Negro demands, but the party was unable to defuse the racial tension sundering the nation. . . . The general opposition which deposed the Democratic party came in large part from prospering Democrats who objected to Washington dissipating their tax dollars on programs which did them no good. The Democratic party fell victim to the ideological impetus of a liberalism which had carried it beyond programs taxing the few for the benefit of the many (the New Deal) to programs taxing the many on behalf of the few (the Great Society).

This bears some resemblance to the Wildavsky-Kristol argument about the trouble with the Great Society. But unlike the neoconservatives of a few years later, Phillips was not advancing a judgment about the success or failure of programs. Rather, he was making a purely political point: the Great Society was bound to hurt the Democrats because unlike the New Deal, it aimed to help lower-class blacks. Phillips saw this as a fissure that had opened between Democrats and their traditional bases of support, working-class southerners and urban ethnics in the North. It was up to Republicans to drive a wedge into the crack.

Liberal analysts invariably cite Phillips as evidence that Nixon won in 1968 on the basis of a "southern strategy," a veiled attempt to woo segregationists. As evidence of this, they point not only to his dense monograph but to Phillips's campaign work with Harry S. Dent. Dent, a nefarious lawyer from Columbia, South Carolina, who had been Strom Thurmond's principal adviser, was the man who discovered Phillips and who tutored Nixon in the semiotics of southern politics. With Dent's help, Nixon was able to signal to white voters that he would not aggressively pursue integration while avoiding sounding like a racist. "It was anti-black, not with passion but with a cool, clear-eyed political cynicism," write Reg Murphy and Hal Gulliver in their 1971 book *The Southern Strategy*.

In addition to down-market southern whites, the key group that turned away from the Democrats was the so-called Reagan Democrats, the swing voters who helped produce a landslide against Jimmy Carter in 1980. Blue-collar, often ethnic workers in the North, they were the sort of people who had benefited from the New Deal and supported the Democrats out of gratitude ever since. According to the liberal version, these voters did not leave the Democratic tent on their own. They were kidnapped by Republican politicians who played diabolically upon their fears and economic insecurities. "Explicit race-baiting was left to Wallace," Democratic pollster Stanley Greenberg writes in his 1995 book *Middle-Class Dreams,* "but there was no mistake about the centrality of race to the new conservatism."

This case focuses attention on Nixon's actions as president. Once elected, the argument goes, Nixon continued to dabble in racial semaphore: he hinted that he would drag his feet on implementating court-ordered school desegregation and weaken the Voting Rights Act. He sent a racial "message" with his Supreme Court nominees Clement Haynesworth and Harrold Carswell, both conservative southern judges. Haynesworth had sided against civil rights as a judge in South Carolina. Carswell had helped convert a public golf course, under order to desegregate, into a whites-only private club. To support this part of their case, liberals must strain to explain Republican policies that on their face look like racial liberalism. For instance, Kenneth O'Reilly, in his book *Nixon's Piano,* contends on the basis of rather thin evidence that even Nixon's promotion of affirmative action was a kind of Trojan horse meant to divide blacks from organized labor.

A more sophisticated version of this argument holds that liberals themselves bear a portion of the blame for the damage done them by racial issues. Thomas and Mary Edsall argue in *Chain Reaction* that working-class whites bore the brunt of liberal policies like busing and affirmative action, especially in the North. Busing, they write, "brought home . . . vividly to whites the image of the federal government as intruder and oppressor—the same government which for millions of voters had for nearly forty years been seen as relatively benign, and often as benefactor and protector." Limousine liberals, it appeared, were re-engineering society at no expense to themselves but at great cost to those who were struggling lower down the economic ladder.

Whether it was Democrats or Republicans who provoked the racial backlash, liberal analysts all castigate conservatives for taking advantage of it. By the 1980s the G.O.P. was conducting politics in a kind of coded language. In this view, "special interests," tied to the Democratic Party, meant blacks. A "liberal" was someone who favored helping blacks. "Taxes" signified the redistribution of wealth from white workers to blacks on welfare. Republican strategist Lee Atwater is credited with being a master at prying Democrats away from their party through the covert use of racial issues: the ACLU; Willie Horton; the death penalty; "Harvard." In *Pledging Allegiance,* an account of the 1988 campaign, Sidney Blumenthal writes, "The Bush campaign virtually nominated Willie Horton as Michael Dukakis's running mate. . . . The Willie Horton videos of 1988 played upon such atavistic racial feelings with even greater consequence than did *The Birth of a Nation.*" Greenberg argues that in order to win the presidency, "Bush shifted to the tactics of Richard Nixon. . . . He stoked the fires of public cynicism in order to allow the Republicans to hold on to the presidency."

Beginning in 1985, Greenberg, who later became Bill Clinton's pollster, made an influential study of voters in Macomb County, Michigan, a heavily Catholic working-class area outside of Detroit. Macomb was an ideal laboratory; it went heavily for Kennedy and Johnson in 1960 and 1964, but only marginally for Humphrey in 1968, and had gone Republican since 1972. It was the spiritual home of the Reagan Democrats. Race was clearly what had impelled their conversion. As Greenberg writes, "The white defectors from the Democratic party expressed a profound distaste for black Americans, a sentiment that pervaded almost everything they thought about government and politics." To them, "Detroit was just a big pit into which the state and federal governments poured tax money, never to be heard from again."

Curiously, these noxious views lead Greenberg—who began his career as a neo-Marxist—to adopt essentially the Phillips critique of Great Society liberalism. Though he describes the residents of Macomb as unregenerate racists, he thinks Democrats need to change in order to recapture their votes. The party did go wrong politically during the Johnson years, he argues, not by failing at government but by favoring the poor and minorities. Greenberg criticizes social programs that focused on the poor, like Community Action, and means-tested programs like food stamps, Medicaid, and subsidized housing. *Means testing* is a dirty word in his lexicon; to him it means more Republicans and fewer Democrats. Social Security, which isn't means tested, has an enduring constituency. The middle class gets something from it. Welfare, which is means tested, has become grossly unpopular because it does the middle class no good. Greenberg thinks what he calls "the end of universality" brought on the liberal downfall. He sees a return to universality as the means to recovery.

What's Wrong with These Pictures?

Both the conservative and liberal arguments begin with nuggets of truth—that liberal social programs developed new and serious flaws in the 1960s, that conservatives have often manipulated racial prejudice for political advantage—and then extend those insights way too far. Conservatives exaggerate the Great Society's failures in order to discredit liberalism's successes; liberals overstate conservative cynicism to gloss over faults of their own.

Among Republican leaders, it is Gingrich who most regularly lapses into hyperbole and distortion in attempting to nail shut the coffin of his opponents. In an expansive mood at one of the daily news conferences he held during the first hundred days, Gingrich referred to the Democrats and "the monstrous death traps they have created, their public housing projects that are death traps for the poor, their public schools that are literacy traps for the poor." Universal public education was a Jeffersonian idea; it dates from long before the existence of the modern Democratic Party. As for public housing, emblematic projects like Cabrini-

Green and the Robert Taylor Homes in Chicago were built in the 1950s with the support of a bipartisan consensus. The legislation that enabled them was actually sponsored by the ultraconservative senator Robert Taft and signed into law by President Eisenhower. Johnson's housing program was Model Cities, an effort to make up for the mistakes of slum clearance. When challenged by a reporter about his assertion, Gingrich fell back to the position that it was federal aid to disadvantaged students beginning under Johnson that made public education "really bad." In housing, he said, the real issue was welfare.

To Gingrich, *welfare* stands as shorthand for all the failures of government. By invoking with a sneer the phrase *welfare state,* he implies that collective action is typified by welfare, a sense heightened by his using the terms *welfare state* and *welfare system* interchangeably. As Gingrich knows, the *welfare state,* as that expression has always been understood, encompasses nearly all of the federal government's involvement in the nation's domestic life—not just AFDC, the program popularly known as welfare, but also Social Security, Medicare, unemployment insurance, crop insurance, pensions, environmental protection, education aid, and the rest. The welfare state costs us about a trillion dollars a year. The welfare *system,* on the other hand, is composed of the joint state-federal program AFDC, the various state programs that supplement it, the federal food stamp program, and Supplemental Security Income (SSI), which goes to the disabled. Combined state and federal spending on these efforts amounts to only about $75 billion a year. But the misunderstanding serves a purpose; it suggests at once that government is terribly expensive, that it focuses mainly on the poor, and that it serves even them badly.

This case against government also demands a strong measure of confusion about what the New Deal and the Great Society actually did. "The official dismantling of President Lyndon Johnson's edifice began at 1:50 P.M. on Friday, March 24, 1995, when the House voted to 'de-entitlize' nearly 50 welfare programs and return the money to the states," Richard Armey noted in a cele-

bratory article. Echoing Reagan and Gingrich, Republican legislators habitually reiterate this line: they are reversing *LBJ*'s failed
project. Rush Limbaugh, in his book *The Way Things Ought to Be,*
quotes himself: "We have the poor and we have poverty in this
country precisely because of the liberal approach, which has been
proceeding full steam in this country since the Great Society."

Folding unpopular programs into the Great Society caters to
the misconception that thanks to Johnson federal resources go
mostly to the poor. Likewise, creating the impression that Social
Security and Medicare come out of another time and another
philosophy gives Republicans an excuse for not demanding their
repeal or "de-entitlization," as Armey might term it. In fact, the
program Republicans most want to deconstruct dates not from
the Great Society but from the New Deal. It was Roosevelt and
his secretary of labor, Frances Perkins, who created the program
that has come to be known as welfare: Aid to Families with
Dependent Children (AFDC), or Aid to Dependent Children
(ADC), as it was originally called. Adding to the irony, ADC was
actually part of the Social Security Act of 1935.

In trying to confuse the New Deal and the Great Society, conservatives also exaggerate the differences between them. In reality, they had far more in common than is usually assumed. Both
lacked careful plans, clear ideas, or a thought-through vision of
what they wanted to accomplish. Both were essentially haphaz-
ard, "a chaos of experimentation," in a phrase Richard Hofstadter used to describe FDR's program. "It is common sense to
take a method and try it. If it fails, admit it frankly and try
another. But above all, try something," Roosevelt said in 1932.
The same spirit, if less openly acknowledged, guided the Great
Society. In his book *The Promised Land,* Nicholas Lemann
describes how seat-of-the-pants the War on Poverty really was.
When Walter Heller, who had been JFK's chief economic
adviser, talked Johnson—against the president's instincts—into
authorizing community action as an approach, the idea "was still
so new that it was completely unclear whether it did in fact work

as a way of reducing poverty," Lemann writes. As Johnson's efforts were getting under way, the Vietnam War intervened, diverting resources and attention from the effort, much as World War II preempted the New Deal.

Conservative intellectuals also distort history when they argue that the New Deal was aimed at a broad public, while the Great Society served only the perpetually poor. In reality, there were New Deal programs that benefited only narrow groups such as dislocated farmers and destitute old people. The ADC program was created for widows with little prospect of ever making a living. Social Security was targeted at the elderly poor. The Rural Electrification Administration and the Tennessee Valley Authority were sectionally based. Conversely, the largest Great Society program was Medicare, which provided health care for all senior citizens. While billions went to expand universal Social Security benefits, the War on Poverty was originally capitalized at a mere $962 million, less than 1 percent of the federal budget at the time.

The commonalities between the New Deal and the Great Society are not coincidental. Johnson saw his program as a culmination of the unfinished business of the Roosevelt and Truman administrations. It would include most of what those presidents wanted but couldn't get Congress to pass: health care for the poor, federal aid to education, housing subsidies, and voting rights for blacks. Johnson understood the political drawback to programs narrowly aimed at the very poor. Community Action troubled him for that very reason. Johnson took care not to target the program at black teenagers for fear the lack of a sufficient base would deprive it of the oxygen of congressional support.

In terms of their efficacy, the New Deal and Great Society both offer a more mixed picture than is generally supposed. The failed programs of the New Deal tend not to be remembered, but there were many of them. The National Recovery Administration, which granted permission to businesses for monopolistic price agreements and production quotas, probably slowed down the recovery, which got going only after the Supreme Court threw out the NRA in 1935. As Alan Brinkley writes in *The End of Reform,* though they complained bitterly, Roosevelt and his cabinet were privately thankful for the Supreme Court's action because the NRA wasn't working and they didn't know what to do about it. New Deal economic policies precipitated a disastrous recession in 1937. In 1940 there were 10 million people, or one in four workers, still unemployed. The reputation of the New Deal as a whole was probably saved by the expansion brought on by the attack on Pearl Harbor.

Conversely, many of the programs that made up the War on Poverty were far from the obvious failures their current reputations suggest. Food stamps essentially wiped out hunger in America at a very low cost. Medicaid and WIC—the Women, Infants, and Children program—led to a significant drop in infant mortality and an increase in life expectancy for the poor. Children enrolled in Head Start are more likely to graduate high school. Increases in Social Security benefits further diminished poverty among old people. Even the flawed Community Action program helped to develop a black professional class and train a generation of black political leaders. In combination, all of these efforts helped to effect a dramatic decrease in the number of people living below the poverty line, from 22 percent in 1960 to 13 percent in 1969. The sharpest decline was in black poverty.

There were indeed enormous failings in the Great Society, failings for which liberals still have much atoning to do. Murray and Gingrich have a point about Johnson and welfare. By 1965 it should have been clear that the program fostered dependency. Instead of grappling with this problem, the Great Society exacerbated it by expanding benefits, fueling a threefold increase in the welfare rolls between 1965 and 1972. FDR was frank about the experimental nature of what he was doing and had the excuse of a national emergency. LBJ, by contrast, was originally responding to what he thought was JFK's legacy. Riots and urban disorder developed as the effort got under way, adding a sense of urgency. But in truth, LBJ faced no comparable demand for immediate action. An even greater fault was Johnson's pitching his programs in a rhetoric so inflated that they couldn't possibly deliver results to match, even if they had been stunning successes. The "total victory" he demanded in his War on Poverty raised expectations that could only be dashed.

But the effort of the Great Society hardly serves as a basis for the kind of generalizations conservatives wish to draw from it. There is no objective way to compare American poverty to what it would be had there been no Great Society. In any case, it would have been no better with Republicans in charge. In those years Nixon and Milton Friedman also advocated expanding welfare generously. Though it deserves much of its reputation for sloppiness and error, the War on Poverty no more discredits the ability of the American government to fight poverty than the Desert One disaster or the Marine barracks bombing in Beirut discredit our ability to fight wars. The argument is compelling only if one believes as a matter of principle that we shouldn't fight them.

As an account of our turn away from government, the liberal version fits the chronological framework better than the conservative analysis. The erosion of public confidence in government corresponds to the Civil Rights Act of 1964 and the reversal of political positions that took place in the presidential election of that year. Rising disenchantment antedates the deployment of the Great Society intervention, and certainly the conspicuous failures that Republicans suggest caused it. As liberals argue, race was clearly a principal lever by which canny conservatives sought to pry those who previously saw themselves as beneficiaries of government away from the traditional party of government. In 1976 Kevin Phillips recommended a Reagan-Wallace ticket as a likely winner for the G.O.P. In 1978 Newt Gingrich won election to the House from his Georgia district for the first time, in part by race-baiting his opponent, Virginia Shapard. A campaign leaflet portrayed Shapard with Julian Bond, the Atlanta-based civil rights leader. "If you like welfare, you'll love Virginia Shapard," it read. Such tactics were a hallmark of Republican politics throughout the South in the 1970s. National Republicans seldom espoused racism or openly opposed desegregation. Yet they had managed to indicate where their sympathies lay.

But liberals who stop there have only begun to explain the reaction of the next three decades. Distrust of government now flourishes in areas that have little if anything to do with race. The notion that government squanders resources in a corrupt and cavalier fashion extends to the Pentagon as well as HHS and HUD. Hostility toward career politicians and the outcry for term limits are phenomena with little connection or correlation to racial views. Blacks too are increasingly skeptical about government and politicians, according to polling data. In the relative success of Ross Perot's 1992 campaign one sees the backlash stripped of any appreciable racial overlay. And indeed, Perot's anti-Washington rhetoric had far greater resonance than Pat Buchanan's racially tinged version.

The liberal interpretation has also been contradicted by events since Clinton took office. On Stanley Greenberg's advice, Clinton carefully tailored his early proposals on a New Deal cut, not a Great Society one. In his health care reform plan, Clinton drew upon the New Deal principle of universality. His program was built around the idea of "security" for all. It offered the middle class a tangible benefit. Little was said about the poor, who were already covered by Medicaid, a means-tested Great Society program. Politically, however, the result was not a return to the success of the New Deal but a failure greater than any before. The problem, Democrats discovered, was not that the public didn't like government programs targeted at the poor or minorities, but that it didn't trust bureaucrats or programs, period—even if, or perhaps especially if, they promised something for nothing. Once Republicans began to attack the Clinton plan as an expansion of federal power into a realm of private choice, they drew a strong response. That this attack found its mark testifies to the political reality of a public so skeptical of large-scale collective efforts that it rejects them out of hand, regardless of who benefits.

If dislike of government now transcends issues of race, so too does Republican politics. The G.O.P. as a whole increasingly seems to be moving beyond racial coding. In 1980 the Republicans held their convention in Detroit; it was a statement that the party wanted black votes. Although it has yet to win over African-Americans in substantial number, the possibility no longer seems remote. Jack Kemp and other "new paradigm" conservatives have staked much on their effort to bring blacks back to the party of Lincoln. The Republican campaigns of 1992 and 1994 were not, to any significant degree, based on racial appeals.

To argue that they were, liberals have had to push the "coding" argument farther and farther. Any discussion of crime or welfare, some on the left argue, is a way of beating up African-Americans. Though there is certainly a racial component to these issues, they are not merely, or even mostly, that. Blacks too regard them as fundamental and valid concerns. In opposing affirmative action, conservatives now strain to argue that abandoning it is a matter of neutral justice, that they only want a return to the color-blind ideal of the civil rights movement. To insist this is merely covert racism denies the possibility of any legitimate opposition to the practice. Faced with the prospect of a black leader, most Republicans do not flinch. When Colin Powell flirted with running for president as a Republican, there was little sense that his being black—as opposed to his being a moderate—would prove an impediment.

For liberals, blaming antigovernment sentiment on racism has become an excuse for their own failure. But voters didn't desert government en masse simply because it was principled on the issue of racial equality and they weren't. Something *has* gone wrong. Despite a long list of genuine accomplishments, there is a real element of bloat, failure, and overload in government efforts of various kinds over the past thirty years. For liberals to attribute this view simply to bigotry and self-interest is as unrealistic as it is for conservatives to ignore what government has achieved. We need a more balanced view, a more complete story.

The Expectations Gap

There are, of course, varieties of antigovernment feeling, each with its own wellspring. Many liberals became cynical about the government, at least for a time, because of executive malfeasance in Vietnam and during Watergate. A cluster of neoconservative intellectuals turned away from the notion of an activist national government because of what they observed as a string of real-world failures. Christian conservatives dislike the values of liberal policymakers and the usurpation of local prerogatives. Libertarians are against government intervention on philosophical grounds.

But what of the person in the street, who is neither instinctively ideological nor much attuned to inductive reasoning about such matters? If he tells a pollster he no longer trusts Washington, it is not because he thinks the War on Poverty wasn't cost-effective, or because Lee Atwater played upon his insecurities. It is rather a response to his own experience of government. For a general explanation of why the mass public has lost confidence, we need to look at what that public has expected and what its government has done, or failed to do, for it.

In the last thirty years a gap has developed between the public's expectations of government and its actual accomplishments. Efforts like the Gautreaux program in Chicago stand out because bold and effective intervention has become the exception, not the rule. Though it is not a matter of striking out instead of hitting home runs, our batting average is down, and badly. But the public bears some blame too. Its demands have been high, and in many cases unreasonable; all problems are now seen, in some sense, as government's fault, or at least government's to solve. Yet there has been, in recent decades, little corresponding willingness to incur financial and social costs. When we want something accomplished, we view government as "us," a cooperative mechanism for getting the job done. When it comes time to pay the bill, however, we view it as "them," a malevolent, external force.

Those who were young during the decades of the thirties, forties, and fifties had remarkably little experience of the federal government's failing at anything. Memories of the Depression and the Second World War instilled in the generations formed by those events a tremendous faith in the power of the American system to answer the most daunting of challenges. Forty years of barely interrupted prosperity fostered the sense that increasing economic well-being was a given. Europeans often remark on what they take to be the naive American faith that all problems have a solution. But that disposition isn't just the expression of some goofy inborn optimism. At least until recently, it was based on the collective national experience.

In the sixties and seventies that experience changed. The United States weathered a series of crises and catastrophes that were either failures brought on by government or problems government was ill equipped to handle. One could draw up a very long bill of particulars, from the Bay of Pigs to the energy crisis, from the inflation of the seventies to the televised explosion of the *Challenger* space shuttle. There were, however, four ongoing crises that functioned as prime movers in discrediting government in the American mind: the war in Vietnam; the welfare explosion and the decline of cities; the long-term slowdown in the economy; and, finally, the decline of routine public services. As a result of these trends and events, by the eighties the government's performance at home and abroad no longer seemed commensurate with its power.

Most Americans blamed government for these ills, or at least for the failure to remedy them. If our government overcame the Great Depression, defeated Hitler, and put a man on the moon, why couldn't it win in Vietnam, fix the cities, perpetuate conditions of growing prosperity, and deliver the mail? This reaction is natural but also somewhat unfair, because it blames government for matters beyond its control as well as for its own faults. In some cases, government became the scapegoat for problems it made no attempt to solve.

The implications of Vietnam for faith in government have

been much remarked upon. The war in Indochina raised, more powerfully than ever before, the question of the morality of American intervention. It also opened a new issue of public integrity; it was Vietnam that gave us the phrase *credibility gap* and made the language of military euphemism a mode of political discourse. If the American public was lied to by its leaders before, it was never in such a systematic and chilling way. But perhaps most devastating for attitudes toward government were the questions of efficacy raised by American involvement. At the time of the Gulf of Tonkin resolution in 1964, hardly anyone anticipated that the United States might be entering a decade-long war that would leave sixty thousand Americans dead. But it was not doubted that whatever fight we were joining, we would surely win. This belief was underscored by the disingenuous pronouncements of Pentagon officials under Presidents Johnson and Nixon. In 1965 and 1966, however, Americans began to wonder whether the most powerful nation in the world could in fact win a war against a poor third-world country. By decade's end, it was clear to most that it could not, or that if it could, the victory would be a pyrrhic one.

America's involvement in the war appears in retrospect as a series of terrible blunders and misjudgments. But the United States did not create the communist expansion in Asia; it tried to stop it. And given the seriousness of the threat to freedom and international security, it is hard to imagine we could have ignored it, though in hindsight that might have been the wisest course. The war was an effort to respond to the overwhelming foreign policy imperative of the day; as such it commanded overwhelming congressional support. That we could not save Vietnam from communism at a politically acceptable cost was not apparent during the first few years of the war. Indeed, it was not until 1967 that the war in Vietnam provoked mass opposition and protest. Our government deserves blame not so much for failing to win as for failing to make the tremendously difficult decision to give up sooner. Still, the war left a syndrome that persisted: a deep reluctance to project American military force or to risk using it.

Vietnam coincided with the emergence of an urban crisis that likewise beguiled our efforts to defuse it. Just as middle America was beginning to congratulate itself on overcoming yet another great evil, segregation, the nation's largest cities exploded. The first riot broke out at a Harlem police station in July 1964, a month after Lyndon Johnson signed the Civil Rights Act. That eruption was almost quaint in comparison to disruptions that broke out over the next several years in Chicago, Washington, Los Angeles, and Detroit. These disorders converted large sections of America's urban centers to charred no-go areas. And like the war, the urban crisis was televised, a point that greatly troubled conservatives such as Harvard urbanologist Edward Banfield, who argued that live coverage of riots encouraged looting and mayhem.

The eruption of the ghettos signaled the emergence of a miasma of related problems: the rise of out-of-wedlock births; endemic unemployment; crime; drug addiction; and gang violence. Previously, it was always assumed that black, inner-city poverty was like traditional poverty: a function of unemployment and underpaid employment. But here was a social catastrophe that went beyond those familiar problems. All of the afflictions of the black lower class seemed to reinforce each other, creating what Daniel Patrick Moynihan famously called, in his 1965 report on the black family, a "tangle of pathologies." Had this disaster remained confined to the ghetto it might have had little effect on the greater public. But the crisis of the underclass ramified beyond its boundaries, manifesting itself in a whole host of new problems: epidemic criminality; the decline of urban schools; and the decay of public spaces. The result was a mass exodus from cities, an erosion of the urban tax base, and a decline in every kind of metropolitan functionality.

American society created this catastrophe in an ultimate sense; it began with slavery and was abetted by a history of racism. But government did not create the underclass through modern interventions such as welfare and public housing.

Though this has become a kind of Republican shorthand, not even Charles Murray entirely believes that. He simply maintains that federal programs were a crucial enabling condition. More dispassionate analysis suggests that government was something closer to a guilty bystander. The Great Society policy changes that Murray believes made things worse in the ghetto were for the most part not directed at the black, inner-city poor. In terms of programs that might really have helped the inner cities, the war on poverty included no public jobs program like the WPA and no efforts to combat the problem of family dissolution recognized by Moynihan. Nonetheless, welfare, in particular, became a public symbol for what was wrong with government. A program that seemed to subsidize indolence, it glared as an example of public policy failing to reflect the nation's values. Liberals have often defended welfare by noting that its costs are low relative to other programs. But the price is not the point; the nature of the expenditure is. If Vietnam undermined America's international confidence, welfare and the underclass made us doubt the efficacy of our domestic efforts.

The third trend was less acute but no less devastating in its long-term consequences: the slowdown of the American economic engine in the early 1970s. This is an event that economists admit they still do not fully understand. Productivity growth, which had averaged nearly 3 percent annually since World War II, dropped to just over 1 percent. Though the economy continued to grow, most middle-class families ceased to experience any appreciable improvement in their standard of living. For some reason, the rising tide John F. Kennedy had described no longer lifted all boats. Between 1973 and 1991 the income of the typical American family went up a mere 5 percent after inflation. And even that feeble increase was accomplished by putting in longer hours, not earning higher pay. Workers who had seen their real incomes increase for forty years felt them stall, stagnate, and in many cases drop in real terms. Ronald Reagan's question in the 1980 presidential debate—"Are you better off now than you were four years ago?"—was a brilliant one in part because that election year was the first in which the majority of middle-class voters could honestly answer "No."

The slowing of economic growth is probably the trend for which government deserves the least blame. As Paul Krugman points out in his engaging book *Peddling Prosperity,* economists have no idea why growth slowed; our knowledge provides no sound basis for countervailing action. "Why did the magic economy go away? The real answer is that *we don't know,"* Krugman writes. The stagnation of middle-class incomes became an issue only in the 1992 election. The Clinton administration is the first to try to address it at all. And here, the attempt has been vastly inadequate to the task. Clinton's schemes to rejigger job training programs and raise educational standards were passed only in truncated form in 1993 and 1994. After taking control of Congress, Republicans marked them for elimination. Should slow growth and the decline of middle-class incomes persist, many will blame government. But the truth is that government almost certainly didn't cause it and hasn't yet tried to do much of anything about it.

But the expectations gap isn't just about grand crises. As government has aimed high in a rhetorical sense, it has increasingly missed low, failing to fulfill universally accepted basic functions: public safety; education; infrastructure; and the delivery of routine services. These are problems that we know lie within our grasp. Federal, state, and local governments handled them quite ably, in general, in the decades before the 1960s.

Nathan Glazer has argued that overambitious social policy and the decline in basic services are related, at least when it comes to city governments. The political crisis of New York, Glazer contended in a 1993 article in the Manhattan Institute magazine *City Journal,* arose when it "stopped trying to do well the kinds of things a city can do, and started trying to do the kinds of things a city cannot do." What it can do well, Glazer asserts, is collect the trash, police the streets, and maintain its facilities. The things it cannot do are accomplish social goals like redistributing income or solve cultural problems like poverty, drugs, juvenile delinquency, and teenage pregnancy. Though his article is about cities, Glazer argues by implication that these are tasks no level of government can perform well.

This is a tantalizing argument because, if valid, it makes clear what government should and should not be doing. If we simply can't fight poverty well, we shouldn't fight poverty. But Glazer isn't persuasive in his assertion that failures in social policy are intrinsic, or that the breakdown in services relates to the rise of grander designs. New York, for example, has had a strong tradition of addressing social ills since Fiorello La Guardia was mayor. Alone among cities, it has its own extensive public housing system dating from the 1930s. Glazer doesn't explain how the decline in basic services might have resulted from an increasing focus on social ills. And indeed, it's not clear that there is a connection. The city's expenditures for basic services have increased at a rapid clip, along with spending on social problems, since the 1960s.

It may be that the decline in the efficiency of public efforts of all kinds has some common causes. Already by the 1960s public institutions of all kinds were exhibiting signs of decay. The principal problem was not the advent of exotic purposes. Rather, it was a kind of weedlike growth; bureaucracy expanded not in response to public mandate but according to some logic of its own. If, by the 1980s, New York City had a gratuitous hundred-car fleet of drivers for its fire department brass and a Brooklyn warehouse filled with nonteaching bureaucrats, the excesses of liberal social ambition had very little to do with it.

The same thing has happened at the federal level. In a phenomenon Paul Light calls "thickening government," public-sector hierarchies have expanded exponentially over the years. In many cases departmental structures became so intricate and convoluted that a low-level employee would have to take sixty or seventy prescribed steps to accomplish a simple function. Ironically, according to Light, the biggest culprits in this process were Herbert Hoover, who chaired a presidential advisory commission that recommended augmenting the hierarchical structure of the federal government in 1949, and Dwight D. Eisenhower, who quietly implemented a vast additional expansion. Such was the fashion in management before the age of Peter Drucker and Thomas Peters.

With bureaucratic expansion came clumsiness and torpor. In the case of government, inertia had two powerful allies, which happen to have been reforms liberals fought for over a period of many years and finally achieved: civil service rules and public-sector unionization. In combination, these phenomena not only diffused public accountability; they ultimately destroyed any practical system of reward and punishment.

One can trace the origins of these problems a long way back. In 1883 Congress passed the first civil service reform, moving the bureaucracy from a spoils to a "merit" system, with hiring based on competitive examination. The reality was, however, that career civil service employees continued to mix with a generous sprinkling of shorter-term political appointees. By the 1960s, however, officials accountable to politicians were becoming a rarity. With the exception of Congress, which preserved its traditional prerogative of patronage, political appointees became a tiny minority in the federal government. Civil servants even infiltrated the top levels of the executive branch. At the end of the Eisenhower administration in 1960, political appointees still occupied 89 percent of 248 top federal executive positions. By 1992, career officials filled 64 percent of the 1,628 slots at the comparable level.

The civil service mania trickled down to every level of government. In Chicago, a liberal lawyer named Michael Shakman brought suit to prevent the use of patronage as a political tool by the Richard J. Daley machine. The 1972 federal order that bears Shakman's name held that city employees could not be made to do political work, nor could they be fired, transferred, or otherwise disciplined for failing to do so. This meant that Daley's successors as mayor, including Harold Washington and Richard M. Daley, had real control over only about nine hundred out of forty

thousand city jobs. The decision remedied a long history of corruption and abuse, consigning to history the legendary cousins
with no-show park district jobs who became columnist Mike
Royko's stock-in-trade. But what disappeared along with these
abuses was a long-established tradition of public accountability.
A Chicago precinct captain in the old days could get a park
cleaned up with Japanese efficiency. Corruption was endemic,
but its benefits as well as its costs were widely distributed. Subsequent decisions hammered home this transformation. In 1976 the
Supreme Court ruled in the case of *Elrod* v. *Burns* that political
firings violated the due process clause, thereby creating rights of
appeal that made it impossible for government employees to be
removed for good reason or bad at any level.

The second change was that public employees won the right
to organize. In 1962 President Kennedy signed an executive
order allowing federal agencies to recognize unions. The states
soon followed suit. Thus, for the past thirty years, public
employee unions have been growing while unionization has
been on the decline for workers of every other kind. Over 40
percent of public employees are represented by unions—nearly
three times the number of private-sector workers who are. Yet it
is private sector workers, who have no other protections and
whose employers stand to gain personally from shortchanging
them, who truly need unions. In the sixties and seventies the
demands of public sector unions actually commanded a good
deal of public support. Thanks to the doomsday threat of withholding basic services, and the fact that the officials they negotiated with were spending other people's money, they won
impressive contracts at the state and local level. From 1980 to
1987, state workers' salaries rose 59 percent, as against 35 percent
in the private sector. Federal unions didn't win the right to
strike, but they did become diabolically effective at using civil
service rules to prevent efficiency and protect their members
from the consequences of poor performance.

The worst consequence for government isn't the generous
salaries and benefits; it's the drag on productivity. As a result of

collectively bargained contracts, public employees have rights of arbitration and appeal that make getting rid of third-rate workers a virtual impossibility. On those rare occasions when a public employee is fired, others have the right to "bump" on the basis of seniority. This initiates a chain reaction, which so disrupts operations that managers are better off ignoring incompetence than trying to deal with it. The combined effect of civil service reform and unionization is a belt-and-suspenders system of protection for public employees. If a clerk at the DMV is surly to you, it is because he rests secure in the knowledge that no matter how much you complain to his superiors, or to your elected representatives, neither you nor they will be able to do a damn thing about it.

Public employee unions have compromised the design as well as the function of government, laying their bodies across the road to block innovation. Throughout the 1980s the National Education Association, the country's largest teachers' union, did all it could to prevent any promising reform: merit pay; teacher testing; public school choice; and most of all giving anyone the ability to eliminate an inadequate teacher or a lousy principal. In so doing, it helped to fuel the public movement for vouchers, a scheme that may undermine public education altogether. AFSCME, the American Federation of State, County, and Municipal Employees, fought tooth and nail to prevent Bill Clinton from reforming the worker training system in a way that would allow competition with dysfunctional unemployment offices. Public employee unions have been strong opponents of meaningful welfare reform, for the same reason. Taking people off the dole to work in government jobs threatens their territory.

Charles Peters, the editor of the *Washington Monthly*, likes to make this point in relation to the post office, an institution that combines the worst excesses of civil service and union protection. In the 1950s, if the mail wasn't delivered on time (and twice a day) you called your congressman. He called the postmaster, who worked under his patronage. If the postmaster couldn't stop the stream of complaints, he would be out of a job. But after the Postal Reorganization Act of 1971, which made the postal service an independent agency, your congressman was likely to be as frustrated as you were. He no longer had the power to make heads roll. Even if he wanted to, your postmaster probably couldn't fix your problem. Thanks to an absurd tangle of union-inspired regulations, managers couldn't move clerks from one job to another, couldn't hire enough part-time or seasonal employees, couldn't contract out for services, couldn't promote, demote, or fire.

This system doesn't even make its well-compensated workers happy, as several hundred thousand grievance filings and a few stress-induced post office massacres attest. The Chicago mail scandal of 1993 afforded a glimpse into the bureaucratic nether-world. As the breakdown of routine delivery on the North Side became national news, hundreds of thousands of pieces of unde-livered mail, some of it eleven years old, turned up everywhere: burned under a railroad bridge; hidden in the back of delivery vans, under a porch, in car trunks, and in the basement of a retired postal worker. After the scandal broke, the officials responsible were transferred elsewhere; there was no question of actually firing them.

As it has declined in quality, postal service has increased in cost. Since 1971 the price of a first-class letter has gone up faster than consumer inflation. For purposes of comparison, the cost of telephone service has risen at less than half the rate of inflation since then; the long-distance companies engage in diabolical competition by sending customers signed checks as bribes to switch services while keeping their rates low. The postal service, on the other hand, has managed, despite its mandate to break even, to lose money most years while raising its rates constantly. The comparison is particularly apt because postal and telephone service were both monopolies, the one government, the other government-regulated, until the early 1970s. Indeed, this seems a case study of why private services are better than public ones—until you remember that the postal service was considered a paragon of courtesy and efficiency for the first 190 years of its existence.

While government has grown less efficient and more expensive, it has also become more arbitrary. In the 1970s the Earl Warren Supreme Court took many of the questions about which Americans felt most strongly out of their hands. Social changes wrought by judicial fiat instead of democratic process made the losers feel cheated as well as defeated. The unhappiness many people felt about school busing, legalized abortion, and the abolition of the death penalty was immeasurably heightened by the fact that there was no civic participation in these decisions. Much of the expansion of government in recent years has followed this model; courts have ordered elected officials to spend money to implement affirmative action programs, remedy unequal school spending, and provide shelter for the homeless. When people speak of government being "out of control," part of what they mean is that the courts and the regulatory process have taken it out of *their* control.

As the costs and the seemingly boundless nature of federal intervention grew, few corresponding gains were visible. Instead of paying for an interstate highway system, or the thrill of a landing on the moon, we were expending more and more to service the national debt and provide generous entitlements that middle-class beneficiaries took to be a natural right.

The way politicians answered this predicament, and the mood it spawned, poured lighter fluid on the bonfire. In essence, government *didn't* respond to the problem of its own growing disrepute; it ignored it. Through the Nixon, Ford, Carter, and even the Reagan and Bush years, federal, state, and local governments continued to expand in an aimless way, gaining weight without ever noticing. They continued to employ more people, take on more tasks, and consume a larger share of national income without any democratic mandate to do so. Between 1980 and 1992 federal civilian employment grew from approximately 2.9 million to 3.1 million. Government revenue at all levels—federal, state, and local—went from $932 billion to $2.26 trillion. Of course, federal spending went up even faster than revenues. Just when it ought to have taken stock and tried to win back its good name, government accelerated its push forward, becoming ever more mystifying, enormous, and, ultimately, insolvent.

It was during this period that distrust in politicians and elected officials became a prevailing sentiment in American political culture. By 1976 pollsters found that 45 percent of respondents said "quite a few" politicians were crooked, up from 24 percent a few decades earlier. In 1992 the figure hit 65 percent. This trend is usually blamed on Watergate and subsequent scandals, and sometimes on the media. But the causality may run in reverse. Viewed in the context of growing mistrust, Watergate, Abscam, Billygate, and a dozen other minigates appear more as symptoms than as breeders of disenchantment. That these scandals appeared in such rapid profusion testifies to the unease already latent in the public consciousness.

A new kind of journalism abetted the development of this attitude. The investigative reporting of the 1970s was principally about government failure and wrongdoing. Unlike the muckraking of the Progressive era, however, it lacked a strong sense of idealism or a reformist ethos. Though journalists like Jack Anderson and Mike Wallace cast themselves as defenders of the taxpayer, their reporting lacked any emphasis on making government work. It helped to tear down institutions without ever telling anybody how to rebuild them.

By chipping away at faith in the instruments of collective action, the new muckrakers paved the way for conservative attacks upon them. Indeed, conservatives learned to adopt the same techniques. The Grace Commission report of 1980, a private study of public waste, was really an exercise in investigative journalism with an explicit bias; horror stories like the Pentagon's $600 hammer were related with the object of making government seem ludicrous and frightening. As Stephen Kelman argued in an article in *The Public Interest* in 1985, these tales were often gross distortions. But even where the legends weren't literally true, they flourished for a reason. Like welfare, they were metaphors for what was wrong with government.

Because of the undercurrent of distrust, political scandals of all kinds were profoundly damaging to government in the seventies and eighties. Previous outrages—Credit Mobilier, Teapot Dome, the profiteering outrages of World War II, the influence peddlers of the Eisenhower administration—brought down individual politicians and sometimes political machines. But they had little effect on underlying attitudes because government was seen to deliver despite the opportunities for corruption it inevitably created. When feelings about government turned sharply negative, however, episodes of illegality ceased to be accepted as a necessary evil; they were taken to discredit the whole enterprise. Today there is surely less outright corruption in American politics than ever before, certainly than in the days when campaign contributions were made in cash and money changed hands on the floor of the House. If the sleaze that remains produces more outrage than ever, it may be because we no longer see our national progress bound up with such misdeeds.

The steady outpouring of journalistic outrage has helped create a vicious circle: cynicism whets the appetite for scandal; scandal feeds cynicism. In such a situation, what the political writer Jean Bethke Elshtain calls the "cycle of delegitimation" takes over. Under such circumstances, failure becomes a self-fulfilling prophecy. Government becomes the Little Engine That Couldn't, undermined by its lack of confidence on top of other problems. For conservatism, this mood has been a great boon. Since Reagan, posturing against Washington has been a crudely effective mode of politics. But for a nation beset by problems that cannot be addressed without the concerted attention and resources of government, such an attitude merely digs the hole deeper.

Chapter Three

THE REPUBLICAN EVASION

The American conservative . . . fills the vacuum where demo-
cratic purpose should be.
— WALTER LIPPMANN, *Drift and Mastery,* 1914

SENATOR John Breaux of Louisiana, a moderate Democrat, tells
of an incident that happened just after the 1994 election. An
elderly woman came up to him at a rally and implored him to
stop the government from taking over Medicare. Apocryphal or
not, the fable well illustrates the misunderstanding that the
Republican attack on government encourages. Government is an
interloper that intrudes, takes things over, and squanders your
hard-earned money on people who have no right to it. Popular
programs like Social Security and Medicare, on the other hand,
are something else again—they're *yours.* To assist people in
despising government, Republicans define it creatively.

The antigovernment ideology of the G.O.P. is something we
now take for granted. But to understand this politics and its con-
tradictions, we have to ask, with apologies to Rudyard Kipling,
how the elephant got its trunk. How did the party of Lincoln,
Theodore Roosevelt, and Dwight D. Eisenhower become the
party of Reagan and Gingrich? How did it turn against government in such an extreme and sweeping way?

Antigovernment feeling is by no means intrinsic to Republicanism. On the contrary, in the latter part of the nineteenth century there was little one today would recognize as conservative about the G.O.P. As against the Democrats, Republicans stood for higher tariffs to protect domestic industry, more generous pensions for Civil War veterans, assistance to war widows and orphans (the nineteenth-century welfare state), and harsher treatment for the defeated South. There was no real disagreement over principle; both parties were committed to laissez-faire as internal economic policy and to an isolationist foreign policy beyond the Western Hemisphere. As legatees of the Hamiltonian tradition, Republicans were, if anything, more ready to use the federal government for what we now would call industrial policy. The Department of Agriculture and the land-grant colleges were projects of the Lincoln administration. If the bearded late-nineteenth-century Republicans are recognizable as forebears of contemporary ones, what links them is simply ingrained bias in favor of the wealthy.

But if antistatism was not a Republican theme in the late 1800s, there was not yet much state to reject. It was William Jennings Bryan who, in the campaign of 1896, first committed the Democrats to expanding the domestic powers of the national government. Not until then was there reason for Republicans to oppose doing so. William McKinley, who defeated Bryan, stands as the first modern antigovernment Republican. But after McKinley was assassinated by an anarchist, his successor, Theodore Roosevelt, disrupted what might otherwise stand as a century-long continuity. Between 1901 and 1909, Roosevelt presided over the most ambitious expansion in the federal role since Lincoln. In the age of giant trusts, the danger to democracy resided not in a too-powerful federal state, as Roosevelt contended in his December 1908 message to Congress, but "in having the power insufficiently concentrated so that no one can be held responsible to the people for its use."

That speech was roundly denounced by Democrats and Republicans as a subversion of the American tradition and even an attempt to abolish the states. But by that time Roosevelt had already transformed the federal government, creating the Commerce Department, expanding antitrust enforcement under the Sherman Act, and directly regulating the strongest commercial power in America, the railroads. Perhaps Roosevelt's most profound achievement was in conservation. "To waste, to destroy our natural resources, to skin and exhaust the land instead of using it so as to increase its usefulness, will result in undermining in the days of our children the very prosperity which we ought by right to hand down to them amplified and developed," he declared. Roosevelt quadrupled the federal government's land holdings and created the National Park Service.

Roosevelt's own chosen successor, William Howard Taft, was something of a throwback to McKinley, more conservative by nature and skeptical of federal action. But thanks to the prodding of the Progressive movement, which was in full flower during his presidency, Taft couldn't reverse course. Instead he added several increments to Roosevelt's economic regulations, sponsoring a law that improved mine safety and assisting in the passage of the progressive income tax, the funding mechanism that made all future social legislation possible. Nonetheless, the increasingly radical postpresidential Roosevelt thought Taft and the Republicans had betrayed his ideas; in 1912 he bolted the party and ran as a Bull Moose Progressive.

Woodrow Wilson ran against Taft and Roosevelt as a traditional Democrat, friendly to states' rights and hostile to the remnants of Bryanism within the party. But with Wilson's inauguration in 1913, federal activism can be said to have made its permanent home among the Democrats. Antistatism now emerged as an exclusively Republican creed. With Roosevelt gone, the G.O.P. stood against such Democratic innovations as the eight-hour day, the minimum-wage law, and prohibitions on child labor, arguing that such matters were none of Washington's business. In reaction to Wilson's internationalism, Republicans turned to hard isolationism, supporting America's entry into the First World War only on Senator William Borah's pretext that they were actually defending American soil. At the end of the war, they denounced Wilson's fourteen points and led the Senate's rebuff of the president over the League of Nations.

The postwar Republican trinity of Harding, Coolidge, and Hoover was fervently anti-Wilsonian and strongly isolationist. But when it came to domestic affairs, the Republican objection to augmenting government's power was muted and equivocal. The three set the pattern, which continued through the Bush years, of opposing expansion in principle but seldom attempting in practice to roll back the handiwork of Democrats. Republicans of the 1920s didn't try to repeal the Sherman Antitrust Act or other economic regulations in the name of free enterprise. They did, however, enforce them only casually. In reality, the difference between the parties in the 1920s was a matter of slower versus faster government growth. Harding made no real effort to repeal the social and labor legislation of Wilson's first term, and in several instances he added to it. So too did Coolidge, who fathered the Railway Labor Mediation Act of 1926 and gave longshoremen and harbor workers compensation for injuries. The philosophy of government Coolidge broadcast was a napping passivity rather than ardent antistatism. "There were no thrills while he reigned, but neither were there any headaches," H. L. Mencken wrote. "He had no ideas, and he was not a nuisance."

Though Herbert Hoover is today remembered as the prototypical arch-reactionary, he was really the most progressive of the lot. Hoover believed in a stiff inheritance tax and wanted to ban child labor (though he thought it took a constitutional amendment to do it). He also approved such interventions in the economy as using public funds to promote exports and fix farm prices. Only after he was out of office, when FDR brought forward the New Deal, was Hoover galvanized by what he saw as a fundamental threat to the constitutional order. Hoover's postpresidential rhetoric left him sounding far less compromising than he was as president.

In the 1930s the G.O.P. was split between Hoover's absolutism and accommodation with the New Deal. The Hooverite view was upheld by Senator Robert Taft of Ohio, the son of the former president. Taft and his faction opposed American entry into World War II until the Japanese attack upon Pearl Harbor. What linked their isolationism to domestic policy was the concern that military expansion would leave the federal government more powerful, as it always had in the past. Taft feared that American involvement in the war would bolster Roosevelt's "creeping socialism." As the leader of Republicans in the Senate through the Roosevelt and Truman years, he expressed an antistatism that was utterly consistent, principled, and for obvious reasons extremely unpopular through the Depression and World War II. Taft was a presidential candidate in every election between 1936 and 1952 but failed each time to win the G.O.P. nomination.

Instead, his party opted for a series of centrist, me-too candidates. But even this strategy availed them little. To invert Harry Truman's aphorism, the public chose a real Democrat over a fake Democrat every time. In 1936 Alf Landon, who only halfheartedly jabbed at the New Deal, was clobbered in one of the most lopsided elections in American history. In 1940 an even more moderate midwesterner, Wendell Willkie, who had been a Democrat until a few years earlier, lost to FDR by a substantial margin. In 1944 New York governor Thomas Dewey, a man with no isolationist taint, got beaten just the same. Dewey came closer in 1948. But the real ideological significance of that election was that Republicans no longer had it in them to challenge the New Deal even at a vague rhetorical level. Too many Americans credited it with bringing them security and prosperity. Dewey had to surrender to Roosevelt before he could run against Truman. By 1950 even Senator Taft looked like something of a liberal.

Republicans finally recaptured the White House in 1952. But the price of success was an almost complete abandonment of conservative principle. No one knew whether Ike was a Republican or Democrat until he declared himself in January 1952; he had no political past, and expressed open hostility toward his adoptive party. Eisenhower called his own philosophy "dynamic conservatism," "progressive dynamic conservatism," "progressive moderation," and "moderate progressivism" before finally settling on "modern Republicanism." The phrase was a euphemism for go-slow New Deal liberalism. Modern Republicans differed from Democrats mostly over the issue of justification: the G.O.P. argued for expanding the federal government's role because of the arms race; they saw a decent social provision as essential to democracy's competition with communism. On this logic, Republicans supported not only the space program but the first federal aid to education, housing projects for the poor, and the interstate highway system, dressed up for the Cold War as the National Defense Highway Act.

Today we remember the 1950s as a "conservative" decade. Despite a Republican in the White House and despite the advent of McCarthyism, however, it was an era that quietly enshrined bipartisan consensus in favor of expanding government. The leading liberal thinkers of the day wrote books pronouncing conservatism defunct. Some went so far as to argue that it had never existed at all. Both Lionel Trilling, in *The Liberal Imagination,* and Louis Hartz, in *The Liberal Tradition,* ventured that there was no significant conservative tradition in America. In place of ideas, conservatives offered only "irritable mental gestures which seek to resemble ideas," as Trilling put it. In his introduction to *The Age of Reform,* Richard Hofstadter posited that liberals like himself were drawn to internal criticism because the conservative side was too minor to bother about. In such a climate, the little band of true conservatives clustered around William F. Buckley's *National Review* could do little more than blow spitballs at a Republican Party that paid them no mind.

The liberal consensus was ratified by the 1960 election, which was almost entirely devoid of ideological content. In the first televised presidential debate Kennedy and Nixon had no real disagreement about the role of government. Though he held some appeal for the right because of his McCarthyite background, Nixon's Republicanism was even more "modern" than Eisenhower's. Notorious among conservatives was the so-called Compact of Fifth Avenue, by which Nixon avoided a convention floor fight by acceding to fifteen conditions set by Nelson Rockefeller. Among its provisions were support for health care for the elderly, civil rights, and aggressive action by the federal government to promote economic growth.

The contemporary strain of antigovernment Republicanism was born in 1964 when Barry Goldwater defeated Rockefeller for the party's presidential nomination. When it came to efforts to improve society, Goldwater broke with Nixon and Eisenhower in favor of the old Hoover-Taft antistatist position. Goldwater wanted to scale back domestic government because he believed it intrinsically destructive of freedom. He opposed not only Social Security, which he derided as "free retirement," but progressive taxation. "My aim is not to pass laws, but to repeal them," he wrote in *The Conscience of a Conservative*. "It is not to inaugurate new programs, but to cancel old ones that do violence to the Constitution, or that have failed in their purpose, or that impose on the people an unwarranted financial burden." Goldwater was essentially a libertarian. He opposed the Civil Rights Act of 1964 not because he was a segregationist but out of a belief that government shouldn't interfere with the right of private association.

Goldwater did not have much immediate effect on his party. Thanks to his embarrassing defeat—the most abject since Landon was sacrificed to Roosevelt in 1936—the lingering antigovernment impulses of his party burrowed deep underground. The lesson Republicans drew from the 1964 election was that they could not challenge the pillars of the New Deal welfare state and thrive. Antistatism became a cult within the party; thereafter, the dominant figures in the G.O.P. were "liberal Republicans," a label that sounds funny in an age when even Democrats don't want to be called that. During the Johnson years, leading members of the opposition acquiesced to the Great Society. Most Republicans supported expanding welfare and Social Security and voted for the new entitlements, Medicare and Medicaid. Some liberal Republicans like Rockefeller, John Lindsay, and Jacob Javits wanted to elaborate the welfare state even more beneficently than Democrats did. In his book *Order of Battle* (1966), Javits argued that aggressive use of federal power was historically more a Republican trait than a Democratic one.

Out of opportunism rather than conviction, Nixon came to embody this brand of liberal Republicanism. Though his southern strategy aimed its arrow at the racial policies of the Democrats, Nixon had little to say about the size of government during the 1968 campaign. His victory was a "negative landslide" in Theodore White's view, a repudiation of Johnson but not a mandate for any alternative philosophy. Nixon advanced far more expansive social policies than any Democrat would dare suggest today, including the most liberal welfare scheme ever proposed by a president, the guaranteed income. Nixon also argued for a system of national health insurance, based upon an employer mandate, and can claim credit for initiating affirmative action. Not only did Nixon not propose rolling back Social Security, he signed a 20 percent increase in benefits and indexed them for inflation. Nixon cooperated with Congress in devising the Occupational Safety and Health Administration and the Consumer Products Safety Commission. He created the Environmental Protection Agency by executive order. The ultimate gambit of Nixon the activist was his scheme to tame inflation through wage and price controls.

The *National Review* crowd was as dismayed by Nixon and Gerald Ford as it would later be by George Bush. But the conservative movement remained a feeble one until it mounted the horse of a new populist movement. When the New Right first appeared on the scene in response to *Roe* v. *Wade,* it was not really antigovernment. Populist conservatives had no aversion to Social Security or Medicare; they remembered FDR and Truman fondly. Their issues were social ones like abortion, school prayer, homosexuality, and pornography. Followers of the Reverend Jerry Falwell objected to the federal government's failure to regulate private behavior in these areas, and even more to liberal court decisions that prevented lower levels of government from doing so. If the New Rightists disliked the continuing expansion of the federal role, it was not because they objected to more government as such, but because it preempted the states from acting on conservative moral principles.

In the 1976 presidential campaign, Ronald Reagan appeared as the champion of the New Right. But in challenging Ford in the primaries, Reagan was weighed down by Goldwater's baggage. Having made his political debut with a nominating speech for Goldwater at the 1964 convention, Reagan was suspected of continuing to share the Arizonan's libertarian extremism. In the primaries, he did little to dispel this impression. Goldwater was "a man ahead of his time," Reagan asserted, who had "tried to tell us some things that maybe eleven years ago we weren't ready to hear." If welfare were to disappear overnight, Reagan claimed on another occasion, no one would miss a meal. Though he tried to distance himself from Goldwater on Social Security, Reagan still emphasized his unhappiness with the system. And when it came to federal spending, he proposed a cut of $90 billion, or some 25 percent in the budget. His program was root canal surgery, deep and painful, and it took him nowhere.

The Reagan Revelation

What created an opportunity for conservatives, and especially for Reagan, was the California tax revolt. Reagan was alert to the political potential of tax cutting early on. In 1973, as governor of California, he supported the budget-cutting Proposition 1, which would have had the effect of lowering taxes. But the poorly drafted measure failed, and it was another four years before the issue resurfaced. When it did, it was with the help of a cranky real estate agent named Howard Jarvis, who had the political insight Reagan lacked: the reason to cut the property tax wasn't to force reductions in spending, it was to cut taxes. Restraining the growth of government would be a fringe benefit.

Proposition 13 ultimately enfeebled California's once-proud system of higher education and left a legacy of decaying public

works and deteriorating services. But thanks to the huge, infla-
tion-fueled budget surplus the state was running at the time, the
initiative did little in the short run to fulfill the dire warnings of
its opponents about cutbacks in services. Proposition 13 made tax
cutting look painless; it gave conservatives an alternative to their
old dour message of austerity. As Robert Kuttner writes in his
book *Revolt of the Haves,* "After decades of unsuccessfully fighting government by opposing the enactment of programs, the tax
revolt suddenly revealed a way to slice through the entire knot."
With Proposition 13, a new Republican vista opened. The tax-
cutting movement said to conservatives that they could quit
attacking the popular heroes Roosevelt and Truman, and instead
hand out free money to voters.

A faction among the Republicans, the supply-siders, really did
think tax cuts meant free money. The basic supposition of Arthur
Laffer, a professor of business economics at the University of
Southern California who had backed Proposition 13, was that
reducing taxes would spur enough additional growth to pay for
the tax cuts without reducing spending. Jack Kemp, former foot-
ball star turned Buffalo congressman, became an evangelist for
this idea even before Proposition 13 passed. In 1977 Kemp took
up the point by proposing, with Senator William Roth of
Delaware, a one-third cut in federal tax rates. In a book published the following year, Kemp made his case. Tax cuts would
act as a magic elixir, stimulating so much economic expansion
that they would pay for themselves. "Tax cuts mean revenue
losses to those who don't understand growth," he wrote. Of
course, if growth made up the loss, the only reason not to reduce
taxes would be spite. Kemp improved upon Jarvis by changing
the mood of the movement from boiling rage to sunny optimism.
Jarvis's book was called *I'm Mad as Hell.* Kemp's was *An American Renaissance.*

Tax cuts fired the Republican imagination. The Republican
National Committee endorsed Kemp-Roth as part of its platform
for the 1978 midterm elections and sent party leaders to tour the
country on a plane called the *Republican Tax Clipper.* One of the

politicians on board was Ronald Reagan. And it was Reagan, more than anyone else, who benefited from Kemp's political discovery. Egged on by his campaign manager, John Sears, and by the success of Proposition 13, Reagan became the first presidential candidate to endorse Kemp-Roth. In 1980 he quit resisting the New Deal. He no longer wanted to make Social Security voluntary or restore Goldwater's reputation. Instead, he ran against the size of the federal government's tax bite. If Eisenhower's philosophy was a modern Republicanism, Reagan's was a distinctly postmodern one. It dressed dowdy old Hooverism in a tax-cut tutu.

In late 1979 Kemp himself was still a potential candidate for president, but few thought him as viable as Reagan. Thus an entente was struck: Kemp chose not to run; Reagan agreed to adopt Kemp's specific tax-cut proposal and to lend his ear to Kemp's supply-side advisers, including a young Michigan congressman named David Stockman. Kemp told Stockman he had successfully converted Reagan to the cause. Whether Reagan was truly converted, or whether he even fully understood the meaning of the term *supply side,* deserves to be doubted. Though he gladly took the Kempites on board, Reagan had a different and in some ways more realistic idea of government's finances. He hadn't really changed. He still wanted to reduce the size of government. "Spending must be limited to those things which are the proper province of government," Reagan said in his first budget message to Congress in February 1981. But he now saw tax cuts as the way to make it happen. Lower revenues would prevent higher spending. In reality they did nothing of the kind. Reagan promised a $100 billion budget surplus in his third year. Instead he delivered a $208 billion deficit.

As the fiscal incoherence of his program became clear, pressure mounted on the administration to find real cuts. For a brief moment Reagan even violated the sanctum sanctorum of the welfare state by proposing to reduce Social Security. But he soon learned his lesson, the same one absorbed by Taft, Coolidge, Hoover, Harding, Eisenhower, Nixon, and Ford: that smart

Republicans never try to turn back the clock on government. Reagan never again made a serious attempt to shrink the big government he railed against. But he was so convincing on the subject of spending cuts that to this day many liberals haven't quite figured out that Reagan wasn't serious.

In 1983 the president signed an enormous increase in the Social Security tax, to guarantee the future viability of the system. Instead of restraining the growth of Medicare, he supported an enormous expansion of the program in the form of coverage for catastrophic care, a bill that was later repealed. Federal spending on social programs went from $303 billion in 1980 to $565 billion in 1989, an increase of 86 percent, as against inflation of 50 percent over the same period. Though he had threatened to eliminate the Departments of Energy and Education, Reagan made his peace with both once in office. Education spending nearly doubled on his watch, from $13 billion in 1979 to $22 billion in 1989. Agriculture spending increased even more, thanks in part to Reagan's new payment-in-kind program. Nor did he get rid of much regulation. Carter had decontrolled trucking, airlines, railroads, stockbrokers' commissions, and deposit interest rate ceilings. All Reagan added was buses and banking.

Why did the Reaganites wimp out? Daniel Patrick Moynihan suggests it was a diabolical antigovernment plot. The creation of the deficit would cripple government prospectively, preempting the development of new programs for decades to come. This analysis probably gives Reagan too much credit and Stockman, who tried his best to cut the budget, not enough. The Reaganites didn't want the deficit, they just didn't face up to it. A more compelling explanation of the Reagan deficits is provided by David Frum, who argues that conservatives simply weren't willing to risk the unpopularity that would have attended trying to unmake massive programs that benefit millions: generous military pensions, farm subsidies, Medicare, and above all Social Security. Insolvency was the path of least resistance.

With George Bush's ascension, inconsistency became blatant hypocrisy. There was no excuse for Bush's failure to fish or cut bait. He had no charm, no curtain of incomprehension to hide behind. Bush understood that the government was spending beyond its means. In another sense, though, Bush was less hypocritical than Reagan. He did make the choice Reagan avoided after a fashion; Bush dropped the charade of pretending to oppose generous government. In 1988 he ran as the education president, the environmental president, and a defender of children. He promoted Head Start and called Republicans the "party of Social Security," and when he ran for a second term he boasted of achievements that included the Clean Air Act and a regulatory supernova called the Americans with Disabilities Act. Though he demagogued against taxes in 1988, Bush did the responsible thing and raised them in 1990. Conservatives would never forgive him, but because of Reagan's previous abdication, they had little standing to criticize. Neither Bush nor Reagan reduced the overall tax burden or the size of government. Through both their administrations, the blob continued to grow.

The G.O.P. Today

Today's Republican Party can be divided any number of ways: pro-choicers versus pro-lifers; the religious versus the secular right; moralists versus the tolerant; free traders versus economic nationalists; immigrationists versus restrictionists; populists versus royalists; economic conservatives versus social conservatives. The common ground that unites these factions is the antigovernment, antitax, antispending line that they all echo to one degree or another. This is the glue that binds Republicans together.

But this apparent consensus conceals a profound distinction. The most important divide in the party is a quiet one over the issue of government, between those who really want to shrink it and those who don't. Within the genus conservative, there are two dominant species: closet libertarians and pseudolibertarians. Closet libertarians like Dick Armey really do mean to shrink the government despite the political costs of doing so. They recognize that Reagan punted, and they want another chance with the ball. You can rant all you want about how Reagan was a fraud, and you won't offend the closet libertarians. They agree with you. Pseudolibertarians like Bob Dole and Newt Gingrich, on the other hand, are Reagan's true disciples. They too use the rhetoric of smaller government but either do so cynically or, like Reagan himself, have no idea what's really involved.

Closet libertarians are the more intriguing cluster. Though they have learned the game of politics, these are not conventional politicians. Many of them have academic backgrounds, mostly in economics. Several are writers. They are inspired by books, but to call them intellectuals suggests a degree of open-mindedness they do not possess. More precisely, they are ideologues, animated by the simple idea of strictly limited government. Closet libertarians are Jeffersonians. The adage that sums up their philosophy is Thoreau's: "That government is best which governs least."

While one can reject this notion of minimalist government, as indeed the vast majority of Americans do, libertarianism is a principled and coherent worldview. It provides an answer to every question. Police departments and the army—yes. Just about everything else—no. Libertarians often come across with a directness that their rivals lack. Ask most politicians, from Gingrich to Clinton, what the role of the federal government is and you'll get a stream of mush. Poke a libertarian and you'll get a clearheaded response. Shortly after he became House majority leader, Dick Armey was asked to define the responsibilities of government. "Defend our shores, build a system of justice, and construct some infrastructure. Gee, I'm running out of other suggestions," he replied. Armey's best-known proposal, a 17 percent flat rate to replace the progressive income tax, is an attempt to produce such a libertarian utopia by the back door. By slashing federal revenues, it would leave Congress with insufficient means to do much beyond the minimum he describes.

But Armey's candor is unusual. Libertarianism remains a philosophy, by and large, that dares not speak its name. Of the leading congressional Republicans who fall roughly into this category—Armey, Phil Gramm, John Kasich, Christopher Cox, and Dana Rohrabacher—only Cox so identifies himself. The word *libertarian* appears nowhere in Armey's 1995 book *The Freedom Revolution,* though it is a (turgid) libertarian tract. When the G.O.P. won control of Congress in 1994, officials of the Cato Institute, the leading libertarian think tank, were ready with dossiers and blueprints on what to slash. But even Cato now euphemistically calls itself "market-liberal," or at least tries to do so.

There is a reason for such reticence. Libertarians cite as their progenitors Jefferson, Alexis de Tocqueville, Adam Smith, and John Stuart Mill, as well as economists of the Austrian school, Ludwig von Mises and Friedrich von Hayek, author of *The Road to Serfdom.* But most Republican libertarians were first inspired not by these nineteenth-century liberals but by the author of *The Fountainhead* and *Atlas Shrugged.* Ayn Rand's philosophy of "objectivism," hyperindividualism tinged with Nietzschean power worship, attracts a number of bookish adolescents after they tire of Hermann Hesse. To call yourself a libertarian thus implies that you were a bright teenager but that you suffer from a stunted intellectual development.

If the Rand connection weren't enough, the loopiness of some self-proclaimed libertarians would surely drive the rest into hiding. Libertarians first emerged as an organized political faction in 1969, when they split off from the conventionally right-wing Young Americans for Freedom (who jeered them out of a convention as "laissez-fairies"). Since then, they have emulated Trotskyists, splitting into ever smaller sects whose differences are comprehended only by a diminishing number of themselves. The biggest cluster in the early seventies was the California-based Libertarian Party, whose Republican origins quickly dissipated into a kind of ponytailed anarcho-pacifism. The party seemed based around the elevation of drug use to a philosophical principle; it made its reputation with a wacky consistency on such issues as "voluntary" funding of defense, abolishing government currency, privatizing sidewalks, and permitting child pornography. It soon turned into a joke on the political process; recent libertarian nominees have included a prostitute named Norma Jean Almodovar and radio entertainer Howard Stern.

Libertarians who aspired to political influence began to distinguish themselves from such frivolity in the late 1970s. The signal event was the Cato Institute's move from California to Washington, D.C., in 1981. Cato originally grew out of the Libertarian Party, but in the last fifteen years has distanced itself, winning considerable respectability and mainstream access in the process. Since the late eighties it has been the most energetic of the right-wing think tanks; after the 1994 election it was also the best connected. When they want to propose the abolition of a few cabinet-level departments, freshman radicals in Congress turn to Cato to find out which departments and why. Stephen Moore, Cato's director of fiscal policy, is a close adviser to Armey and the author of the party's post-Contract platform, *Restoring the Dream.*

But Cato's striped-tie conformity with the mores of Washington hasn't quite assuaged the suspicions of conservatives. Libertarianism is a philosophy that implies, after all, not only that taxes should be low, that the post office should be private, and that AMTRAK and PBS should sink or swim on their own, but that victimless indulgences—drugs, pornography, gambling—are no business of the state's. Such a view does not have to imply vice but in reality remains associated with it. Every so often a Republican will reveal his libertarian leanings by getting caught doing something rather unconservative, like trying to dance onstage at a Grateful Dead concert (John Kasich), financing a porn film (Phil Gramm), or taking drugs and hanging around with heavy metal musicians (Dana Rohrabacher). When Robert Bauman, a socially conservative Maryland congressman, was caught in a tawdry sex scandal in the early 1980s and as a result came to grips with his homosexuality, he realized that he was actually a *libertarian* conservative.

But the problem libertarians have in the Republican Party isn't just their proclivity for sex, drugs, and rock and roll. There is a profound variance between their vision and that of conservatives. Libertarians exalt personal liberty as the summum bonum of politics. They do not think in terms of community; the individual is their largest unit of measurement. Libertarians are congenial to liberals because of their belief that the state should have nothing to say about morality or private behavior. But for the same reason, they are poison to true conservatives, who exalt tradition, order, and virtue. Conservatives want the state to forbid everything libertarians want it to ignore. As Russell Kirk wrote in *The Conservative Mind*, "Libertarianism, properly understood, is as alien to real American conservatives as is communism."

Even when it comes to capitalism, libertarians and conservatives disagree. The libertarian salutes capitalism as a dynamic, revolutionary force. The conservative, by contrast, merely surrenders to it for want of an alternative. He worries, if he has any thoughtfulness at all, about the destructive effects of the marketplace on morality and community. Thus George Will in *Statecraft as Soulcraft* argues for "putting economic argument in its place." The job of government is not leaving each to his own but rather, as he puts it with his usual pomposity, "the improvement of persons."

The reaction of conservatives to even moderate libertarianism, openly expressed, may be gauged from the career of Bill Weld. Weld, the governor of Massachusetts, is an out-of-the-closet libertarian. This gives him no trouble with the tolerant Republicans in his state and attracts liberal votes. But because he supports the right to abortion and has no problem with homosexuals, he has become anathema to the socially conservative majority within the national party. This has turned Weld into a nonprospect for the presidency. Though he might fare well in a general election, he stands no chance in a Republican primary outside of a few liberal states.

Libertarians have absorbed the Weld lesson. Thus the movement may best be understood—like the communist parties of the 1930s—as having both an open and a clandestine membership.

Most but not all the congressional libertarians named above believe drug laws are folly and that the Civil Rights Act of 1964 was unconstitutional. But they are secret members and thus do not break the taboo against saying such things. Milton Friedman and William F. Buckley, who don't have to run for anything, are free to express these views. Robert Bork became a closet libertarian during his Supreme Court confirmation hearing in 1987, when he disavowed his oft-expressed belief that civil rights enforcement was an infringement on the First Amendment freedom of association. With his political career at an end, Bork can openly espouse libertarian views once again. Phil Gramm, on the other hand, cannot. When it comes to social issues, he avers that he is no good at moralizing. The phrase itself is a giveaway; only libertarians consider it moralizing. To conservatives it's morality. In the fall of 1995 Gramm was happy to speak at a Republican conference in Las Vegas, as was Gingrich. True conservatives Pat Buchanan and Richard Lugar wouldn't appear because they objected to the site.

The mutually advantageous alliance with conservatives directs closet libertarians toward economic issues and focuses their attention on the federal government. In those areas there is little disagreement. But in applying their philosophy selectively, they become rather absurd figures. Like Armey, they attack federal intervention on behalf of the poor, but not efforts to impose prayer in the schools. Like Gramm, they defend the Second Amendment more forcefully than the First. Like Christopher Cox, they argue for equal rights—except for homosexuals who want to serve in the military. Electoral politics has a way of making libertarians into hypocrites—or retired politicians.

Even when it comes to basic issues of government spending, libertarians must hide what they really believe. By definition, they reject the foundation stones of the welfare state—veterans' benefits, Social Security, Medicare—all of what Theodore Lowi, in his classic work *The End of Liberalism,* called "the Second American Republic." They cannot, however, oppose these programs openly; to do so would be political suicide. Open repudiation of the Second Republic was the reason Barry Goldwater got only 37 percent of the vote in 1964. It is the reason Republicans still carry the baggage of having once opposed Social Security. Libertarianism violates what is still, in an antigovernment age, a national consensus about what government must do. While they can talk in general terms about less intrusion and scaling back specific programs, libertarians cannot present their full vision of the good society. They are to be pitied, perhaps, for never being able to explain what they believe.

Curiously, as the closet-libertarian minority pretends to be less opposed to government than it really is, the majority faction does just the opposite. As the name implies, pseudolibertarians echo antistatist ideas. Listening selectively to the statements of Dole and Gingrich, one might come away with the idea that they are in fact libertarians. As a group, pseudolibertarians emit a constant chirp about shrinking government; making it cheaper and less powerful; chopping it up and handing it back to the states. At the same time, their actions belie this emphasis. A draft report of the House Republican welfare task force that was leaked to the *Los Angeles Times* suggests Gingrich wants to abolish the liberal welfare state only to replace it with a conservative welfare state of his own. The plan includes funding for one hundred "economic opportunity zones" and turning the earned income tax credit, which goes to the working poor, into a direct cash payment. When a new problem arises that troubles pseudolibertarians, they tend to respond reflexively, just like liberals, with new laws, new programs, and new spending. In reality, pseudolibertarians are practitioners of big government par excellence. Think of them as vegetarians who eat meat.

Self-contradiction is in fact a defining trait of their politics. Pseudolibertarians champion states' rights one minute and vote for federal override of the most basic local prerogatives the next, as in their crime bill, which would deny federal aid to states that decide not to adopt mandatory minimum sentences. They describe general principles, like block grants, then fail to apply them in the case of popular programs like school lunches.

They live with magnitudes of inconsistency that would keep any self-respecting antistatist up nights, railing against unessential government while supporting projects like the superconducting supercollider. But they remain untroubled because their involvement in politics is not based on the pursuit of principle. Pseudos, on the whole, have less intellectual edge than the closets. With the exception of Gingrich and a few others, they are not much interested in ideas, though they often pay lip service to the idea of ideas. Instead of not being able to say what they really want to do, they avoid doing what they say. Their great influence is Reagan. With no Cold War as a justification for overspending, however, their failure to shrink government is even more of an abdication than his was.

There are actually two subspecies of pseudolibertarian: radicals and moderates. The ones who sound most antistatist are the radicals. This group is led by Gingrich and includes the Newtoids, his followers. The most prominent are Gingrich's choices for leadership positions: Tom DeLay, Robert Walker, Bob Livingston, Bill Paxon, and John Boehner. These lieutenants are backed up by a majority of the House freshmen who ran on the Contract with America and were elected with the help of Gingrich's organization, GOPAC. There are a smattering of radicals elsewhere: Rick Santorum and Trent Lott in the Senate, and, somewhere in Indiana, Dan Quayle.

There is a collective profile that applies fairly well to this group. To begin with, by and large they are men. They are white. They come, in the main, from the South and the West. Almost all are in their late forties or early fifties. Thus they share the experience of having been young during the 1960s. Most attended provincial or sectarian colleges where recreational drugs were fewer and sexual experiments farther between. But even at such institutions they defined themselves in opposition to political radicalism and countercultural experimentation. Gingrich alone among them has admitted to trying marijuana. Though most avoided the draft, they supported the Vietnam War. Instead of finding themselves, they married young and went to work.

Reaction against the 1960s continues to form a dominant theme in their politics. At times they seem like a grown-up group of unpopular high school kids. Their instinct to even the score with the in crowd tends to outweigh their more superficial and recently developed urge to shrink government when the two come into conflict. The radicals take more readily to such moralistic ideas as conditioning welfare on marital status or putting churches in charge of it than to sweeping libertarian proposals like eliminating welfare altogether. They are more apt to vote to create a new category of federal crime than they are to remind themselves of their belief that crime is a local problem. The radical pseudolibertarians are also in the forefront of bills to restrict abortion (though many have expediently dropped this), flag burning, and pornography, and to encourage prayer in schools— all at the national level. They wanted federal censorship of the Internet before most of them knew what the Internet was. But to take these as points of contradiction to their antigovernment philosophy gives them too much credit. Unlike closet libertarians, pseudos have no antigovernment philosophy, just a veneer of antigovernment paneling.

More than anything else, the radical pseudolibertarians are defined by Gingrich, surely the most fascinating political figure to come along since Reagan. An eclectic dabbler in disparate traditions, Gingrich doesn't fit easily into any traditional political category. A former professor of history (as he constantly reminds audiences), he is most comfortable in a didactic mode, where he simultaneously defends his positions, excoriates his enemies, and recommends extra reading. Gingrich is often arrogant and testy, especially when vexed by the press or critics, but is nonetheless oddly magnetic. There is no politician of either party who gives more stimulating speeches. Part of Gingrich's appeal is his own wide-ranging curiosity. In a phrase, he jumps from Tocqueville to the Tofflers, from Isaac Asimov to Adam Smith. His political views combine strains of entrepreneurial "new paradigm" thinking, supply-side economics, neoconservatism, and gleanings from science fiction.

When it comes to government, Gingrich's views are deeply equivocal. His mission in life has been trying to lead congressional Republicans into the promised land of majority status, and to that end he has adjusted his opinions continually. The Newt Gingrich elected to Congress in 1978 still carried vestiges of a more liberal past. In his two previous campaigns he had argued for closing loopholes to make the rich pay their fair share of taxes, and attacked his opponent for blocking environmental regulations and not bringing home enough pork-barrel projects. Though he drew closer to the New Right in the early 1980s, Gingrich continued to believe that his party needed to modernize itself by dropping the vestiges of Goldwaterism. In 1983 he told a reporter from the *New York Times* that Republicans suffered from what he termed "a maniacal antigovernment belief" passed on by Herbert Hoover.

His own ideas provided an example of how to transcend that mind-set. Gingrich's book *Window of Opportunity,* published in 1984, argued that the United States should be the first to colonize space. Republicans had missed an enormous opportunity after the lunar landing in 1969, he argued. President Nixon ought to have "announced a massive new program to build a permanent lunar colony to exploit the Moon's resources." This underscores Gingrich's occult side, to be sure, but also his subcutaneous statist instinct. On matters about which he is passionate, his federal aversion abruptly vanishes. Early in 1995 Gingrich was much ridiculed for his idea to help out inner-city blacks with government-subsidized laptop computers; after the laughter subsided he returned to it.

This contradictory attitude befits a legislator who represents Cobb County, a prosperous suburban jurisdiction that ranks third among districts in federal dollars returned per resident, according to a 1993 article in *Common Cause Magazine.* According to the *Atlanta Constitution,* the federal government spent $4.4 billion in Cobb County in 1994, some $10,000 per resident, or nearly twice as much as it spent in New York City. The largest amounts come in the form of defense contracts, small-business loans, and the entitlement programs Social Security and Medicare. Gingrich surely knows how well his constituents do by government, but he has nonetheless encouraged the illusion that public money flows mostly to the poor—through programs like welfare to places like New York, which he calls "a culture of waste."

In the past, Gingrich seemed to have a better appreciation of the reality that cutting government drastically would hurt people who vote for him. As recently as 1992, he wasn't even talking about less government. Gingrich wanted to cast the Republicans as simply more efficient than Democrats. At his behest, the party included a phrase in its 1992 platform promising to "transform the bureaucratic welfare state into a government that is customer-friendly, cost-effective, and improving constantly." His own convention speech was about making government more like Wal-Mart and UPS. This is still his instinct. If you wake him up in the middle of the night and tell him there's a fire somewhere, Gingrich still wants government to put it out. After the Oklahoma City bombing, Gingrich immediately voiced his support for increasing the surveillance powers of the FBI. Armey, by contrast, struck the consistent libertarian note that government had enough power, a position Gingrich adopted only upon reflection.

There is nothing intrinsically hypocritical in a Republican wanting strong federal government. The party's greatest presidents, Lincoln and Theodore Roosevelt, desired exactly that. The problem is that Gingrich has in the last couple of years grown increasingly strident in his articulation of antigovernment sentiments. "We are in the declining phase of a failed welfare state," he often notes. Weeks after the Oklahoma City bombing, Gingrich asserted that popular fears of federal power were "well justified." In his disappointing book *To Renew America,* he links the idea of "big government" to Lenin and Mussolini. "Politicians and intellectuals everywhere were attracted to the idea that their power and intelligence could put them in control of other people's lives and wealth, which could then be used to great purposes," he writes. Curiously, one of Gingrich's heroes is Kemal Atatürk, a dictator of the same era.

Gingrich's wild inconsistency can flourish in a single speech, like the one he delivered to the Association for a Better New York in March 1995. "The welfare state has failed and it has failed in its most basic requirement," he began. "How can any American look at local television news and watch the rapes, the murders, the child abuse, the spouse abuse, the ignorance, the drug addiction, and have any conclusion except that the thirty-year experiment in a federally controlled redistribution system run by bureaucrats is a failure? It is a failure at the level that matters. It is destroying the children." But a few sentences later, Gingrich was denouncing those who had accused him of meaning to cut welfare programs. Over five years, he noted, Republicans were proposing to raise social spending from $842 billion to $1.03 trillion, as against the Democrats, who wanted to spend $1.096 trillion. That people thought programs were actually going to be cut was the result of a media disinformation campaign. "What you have is a Washington press corps, Washington lobbying community, and Washington liberals banding together to defend Washington bureaucrats and shamelessly, shamelessly lying and exploiting children," he added, red-faced and puffing. "Tell us how you really feel," someone shouted from the ballroom floor.

There's a disconnect here. If the welfare state, by which Gingrich means welfare, is destroying American civilization, why not abolish it? This is the view of Murray, Olasky, and Magnet, the social thinkers Gingrich so often cites, and he frequently implies that he shares their views. So drastic a step as actually ending welfare, however, has little public support. It conjures all the symbols of Republican hard-heartedness that Gingrich has no desire to revive: Hoovervilles, soup lines, and the rest. The solution he proposed in 1995 was to hive the whole problem off on the states; let the federal government continue to pay, but remove it from a position of substantive responsibility. It hardly needs to be said that such a compromise is a betrayal of his professed beliefs; if welfare is corrupt and evil, giving a bit less through an intermediary hardly removes the taint. It is the solution of a cynic, one who flourishes by slandering his enemy without actually fighting him.

To Gingrich such a fandango comes naturally. His followers have to be taught the steps. Occasionally one catches a glimpse of the choreography being taught to the baby elephants in dance class:

> Eliminate entire departments, but soften opposition with assurances that "truly important" programs will survive. . . . Be ready with assurances that any "truly important" program will be maintained even while entire departments are being eliminated. . . . Individual programs have friends. Bureaucracies and bureaucrats don't. Therefore, focus the general rhetorical attack on the "Washington bureaucracy." . . . Every budget statement by every Republican official should include the words "cutting the Washington bureaucracy."

Those are the lessons of Frank Luntz in a memo to the Republican conference which was leaked at the start of the new Congress. Luntz is a follower of the zeitgeist; he worked for Pat Buchanan in the 1992 New Hampshire primary, then very briefly for Ross Perot, before signing up with Gingrich and helping market-test the phraseology of the Contract with America. His own politics are nonexistent; he prides himself on serving as a conduit for the vox populi. In the memo, Luntz goes on to explain that his focus-group participants didn't mind the elimination of the Department of Education. It was just the department's biggest program—student loans—that they were afraid of losing. Thus Luntz suggests doing away with the department but keeping its major functions. Here we have the pseudolibertarian creed at its most bald. Talk about cutting government, Luntz recommends, but for God's sake don't really do it. He likes the clang and thunder of a revolution but suggests it be produced by banging on steel sheets.

The hypocrisy of the rival subset, the moderate pseudolibertarians, is either greater or less depending on one's perspective. This group consists largely of people who had little problem with big government until the day before yesterday. These are the successors to the old liberal Republicans or Rockefeller Republicans. Yet ambitious members of the group, like Bob Dole, Lamar Alexander, Pete Wilson, Arlen Specter, Richard Lugar, Jack Kemp, and Christine Todd Whitman, flee such designations like deadly viruses in an age when the only good Republican is a conservative Republican. As against the radicals, the group profile is older, less male, more northern and eastern (or at least not southern), better educated, better dressed, more secular, more affluent, and more divorced. These are Republicans who don't scare liberals; they don't ask for a glass of milk at a dinner party. None was excessively disappointed by the presidency of George Bush. In private, they say nice things about him.

Most of the moderates have spent long careers in government; they date from the era when the antiquated idea of public service held sway and a broad consensus favoring a strong federal social role still obtained. They tend to be pro-choice with qualifications, environmentally concerned, and sympathetic to limited gun control. By their actions, if not their words, they acknowledge that government has an important role to play. As Bush's education secretary, for instance, Lamar Alexander extended Washington's helping hand and ignored the alternative of vouchers. Now he denounces "the arrogant empire" of "hypercentralized," "coercive," and "monopolistic" federal government and supports vouchers. His futile conversion from moderate Republican insider to a populist Beltway-basher in a lumberjack shirt was one of the more amusing episodes in the early presidential jockeying of 1994 and 1995. Another case in point is William Bennett, a moderate-turned-moralist who made his reputation running two agencies, the National Endowment for the Humanities and the Department of Education, which are to true conservatives what gin and whiskey were to the Women's Christian Temperance Union. When he was working his way up the party's patronage ladder, Bennett had no principled aversion to these functions of the federal government. Now he visits congressional committees to call for their abolition.

Many of the moderates are uncomfortable with their party's drift these days. The Nancy Kassenbaums, William Cohens, and Mark Hatfields of the Senate avoid gratuitous government-bashing themselves and grimace slightly when they hear it from others. In the main they are still simply operating by the rules they learned decades ago, endeavoring to bring home new facilities and pork-barrel projects. A case in point is Pat Roberts, a moderate pseudolibertarian from Kansas who has struggled to defend the food stamp program—for the sake of wheat farmers.

Such figures, despised by the new House Republican powers that be, look like old-timers on their way out. Many moderates announced plans to retire in 1996, often citing a declining "civility." Some moderate pseudolibertarians, however, are young and active like Christine Whitman, a star pupil in this class. Born to the squirearchy of western New Jersey, Whitman can trace her lineage back to the Puritan settlers. Though young enough to have experienced the sixties, Whitman reacted to the period not with revulsion but with an extra potent blast of Rockefellerian noblesse oblige. After working in the War on Poverty's Office of Economic Opportunity, she tried to help the G.O.P. figure out why the party was losing blacks and young people. This involved her in such episodes as a meeting with a Chicago street gang called the Black Disciples, whom she apparently failed to recruit. In the 1980s Whitman was regarded as a lightweight. Then in 1990 she discovered antitax politics and surprised everyone by nearly taking Bill Bradley's Senate seat away from him.

In 1994 Whitman added a garnish of antigovernment rhetoric and got elected governor of New Jersey. "Our principal problems are not the product of great global economic shifts or other vast, unseen forces," she said in her 1994 inaugural address. "They are the creation of government." Whitman immediately began phasing in a promised 30 percent tax cut, which made her a hero to conservatives nationally, especially in the wake of the Bush betrayal; she became the first among the promise keepers, a trend that blossomed in the Contract with America. Within a year of her swearing-in, there was talk of Whitman as presidential material. Republicans put her forth as their standard-bearer to deliver the response to Clinton's State of the Union speech in February 1995. "In elections all across America, the voters have chosen smaller government, lower taxes, and less spending," she said. "They have rejected the tyranny of bigger and bigger government, the frustration of one-size-fits-all answers. In a word, they have chosen freedom." In New Jersey, Whitman explained, she had "lowered state spending, not recklessly but carefully and fairly."

There was one problem with Whitman's words: they were totally untrue. In her first two years in office, New Jersey's budget went up faster than the rate of inflation, from $14.85 billion in 1994 to $15.5 in 1995, and $16 billion in 1996. The figure is higher still if you count current expenditures funded through off-budget borrowing. New Jersey's government is growing, not just in absolute terms but as a share of the economy. Hemmed in by her promise to cut taxes and her unwillingness to attack any major category of spending, Whitman has had to turn to a variety of one-shot revenue sources and other gimmicks to maintain balance. Her budgets have relied heavily on reducing contributions to the state pension fund. This simply shifts the liability to future generations. Asked, in a 1994 interview, about the absence of real cuts, Whitman was apologetic and promised that her second budget would be better. In the event, it was more of the same. In her 1995 budget address, Whitman bragged about her many increases in spending, $41 million more for higher education and a 40 percent rise in spending on transportation. As one of Whitman's advisers explained, she was simply too much of a softy to make real cuts. But in November 1995 she once again warned that her *next* budget would contain real cuts. When it arrived in January 1996, it included tiny reductions, accompanied by more juggling tricks.

Whitman's governorship amounts to a replay of Reaganism at the state level. Though she hasn't cut anything much, her rhetoric alarms liberals who take her at her word. Thus there have been howls of protest about Whitman's shifting burdens onto the local level, causing local property taxes to increase. In fact, as she maintains, increases in local taxes are not much related to her tax cuts. There haven't been any reductions in state aid to localities except for a minor penalty formula meant to encourage schools to cut their administrative costs. What Whitman does not point out to her antagonists is that instead of cutting local aid she has funded her tax cuts by borrowing from state pension and trust funds. Yet few Democrats realize that Whitman's call for smaller government is just talk. Thus she finds herself in the *echt* pseudolibertarian position of boasting about downsizing government while simultaneously denying she has cut anything meaningful.

THIS TAXONOMY encompasses the vast majority of active Republican politics. There is, however, one significant minority that doesn't quite fit in the scheme: authoritarians. Authoritarians are true conservatives who have no natural inclination to bother about the size of government; like the New Right from which they emerged, they are worried instead about the soul of the nation. Moral questions, not budgetary ones, quicken their heartbeats. Ralph Reed, Bill Bennett, Alan Keyes, and Pat Buchanan could care less how much Washington spends on NASA, whether it restricts the use of wetlands or lowers the capital gains rate. Their goal is getting government to act in accordance with traditional values, whether it costs more or less.

This leaves authoritarians oddly out of sync with the G.O.P. today. Contemporary Republicanism is now defined by its attack on the size and scope of government and breaks down according to its levels of insincerity. Authoritarians are sincere about morality but ambivalent about government. In fact, most would like to see government do more to safeguard and improve the virtue of the community. Thus despite constant efforts to demonstrate their power, authoritarians have been irrelevant to most of what has gone on in the 104th Congress. In a few instances they have openly broken with parts of the Gingrich program. In the fall of 1995, for example, Buchanan distanced himself from Republican budget cuts in Medicare, which he deemed too harsh. Like other authoritarians, he dislikes government where he believes it undermines morality, as in the case of welfare or grants to artists or census bureau sex surveys. Buchanan has said his first act as president would be to "fumigate" the offices of the NEA. But where government merely helps average people out, he thinks it ought to be left alone.

Why, then, have Buchanan and other authoritarians allied themselves to the Republican revolution? The main reason is that they see themselves accomplishing more by shrinking federal power than by increasing it. To them, Washington is irredeemably liberal and preempts the assertion of moral authority at a lower level. Authoritarians dislike the feds, especially the federal courts, for not letting local governments restrict abortion, homosexuality, pornography, adultery, and the content of school textbooks. For most Republicans, devolution means less government. To authoritarians, however, it really does mean handing power to the states. They think it will promote virtue if Washington steps aside and lets states express the values of their local communities.

The antifederalism of the authoritarians creates the basis for a tactical alliance with closet and pseudolibertarians. Libertarian Republicans also wish Washington would step aside. On education, for instance, they agree that the federal government should keep away. But at the local level, their views diverge. Authoritarians want Washington out so they can Christianize schools and purge Judy Blume from the library. Libertarians, by contrast, are fervent believers in the separation of church and state and enemies of censorship. Libertarians simply want to end welfare; authoritarians are divided on the issue because they see an increase in abortion as one probable consequence of a cutoff. All sides were more or less mollified by Gingrich's block-grant solution, but the broader conflict is far from resolved. The more the common enemy in Washington recedes, the more the battle shifts to the states. And at that level, there's no compromise. Should states end welfare, which will serve as an incentive to abortion? Should they create a requirement to work, which doubles as a prohibition on mothers staying home with their kids? Once power is devolved, there's nowhere to pass the buck. There are analogous splits between libertarians and authoritarians over abortion, pornography, and homosexuality, all equally insoluble at the local level once Washington butts out.

Libertarians and authoritarians can walk together as far as the bridge. But cross it and they find themselves in their naturally antagonistic positions: libertarians pursuing their romantic vision of a nation defined by individuality and freedom, authoritarians pursuing theirs based on community and morality. Should the federal government ever actually forswear its role in education, radicals and authoritarians would join forces in promoting school prayer while libertarians would join moderates in opposing it. This fight would be uglier for its class dimensions. Patrician libertarians would be appalled by the uncouth behavior of populist authoritarians, as they were in the 1970s. Fever-swamp populists would remember their dislike of the eastern establishment.

The Coming Republican Crack-Up

Because of these internal divisions over the role of government, almost any action can threaten the Republican coalition. To take decisive steps against social programs or environmental regulations risks alienating moderates. Not doing so infuriates the freshmen radicals. Restricting abortion upsets closet libertarians. Ignoring it enrages authoritarians. In the first year of the revolution, the Republican Party displayed a unity and an ostensible singleness of purpose that Democrats could only envy. Ronald Reagan's eleventh commandment—Thou Shalt Speak No Ill of Another Republican—hasn't been repealed yet. But examined close up, the alliance is fraught with tensions. Indeed, the most interesting political fight in the period since the 1994 election has been not the battle between Democrats and Republicans but the mostly sub rosa one among the constituent elements of the Republican coalition.

Gingrich has so far acted deftly to quiet internal conflicts and keep the army marching forward. Part of the strategic shrewdness of the Contract with America was its appeal to all the party's factions. No Republican of any variety dares object to a constitutional amendment requiring a balanced budget, deportation for "criminal aliens," victim restitution, a "Sexual Crimes Against Children Act," a "Family Privacy Protection Act," tort reform, forcing Congress to obey its own laws, or a ban on placing American troops under United Nations command. Most of the Contract was symbolic action, with little effect. But in any case, it carefully skirted the party's split on social issues and steered clear of a direct assault on anyone's cherished programs. In this sense, Gingrich's passage of the Contract was a deceptively difficult task, like a circus weightlifter hefting a plaster barbell.

Through this show of strength, Gingrich and the party leadership attempted to build actual unity within the G.O.P. From a distance their discipline looked impressive, especially when compared to that of the Democrats, who proved themselves capable of being as fractious out of power as in. Upon closer inspection, conflict was present from the first. One of the first acts of the Republicans upon their assumption of congressional power in 1995 was to vote a $16 billion "recission" package of cuts in the current year's spending. This was supposed to be a modest down payment on the shrinkage to come—and modest it would have been, since the Republicans needed $1 trillion plus in cuts over seven years to achieve a balanced budget and pay for tax cuts. Instead, the effort underscored just how hard deep cuts were going to be.

Moderate northeastern Republicans threatened to **bail** out over minor reductions in education spending and the removal of funds for new federal buildings in their districts. Even the minor cuts in social spending contained in the bill had to be swaddled in a cushy layer of new largesse: a $7.2 billion bailout for disaster victims in California and Louisiana and assorted other programs. The Republicans were going after the welfare state with a feather duster. When Clinton vetoed the bill on the basis of cuts he didn't like, Republicans criticized him for blocking the new *spending*. "It would be a major mistake for President Clinton to veto a bill that does all these good things," Gingrich said. The Contract indicated a powerful cohesion within the G.O.P., but the recision package suggested the party would not function so effectively when it attempted to move on fundamental issues.

The Contract and the recission package were mere prelude to the great game playing out behind the scenes—the battle of the 1996 budget. On one side were closet libertarians and radicals, who either truly wanted to slim government or saw a political imperative for living up to their promise to do so. They hoped not just to get rid of the Department of Education but to cut back or eliminate student loans. They actually meant to end crop subsidies. In the House, the leader of this camp was the new budget chairman, John Kasich, who indicated his utter seriousness, saying his party would deserve to be thrown out if it didn't fulfill its responsibility to balance the budget. On the opposing team were the moderates who meant to go about their business as usual, if slightly more quietly. The latter camp was leaderless and disparate, but potentially larger in number. Kasich and his followers wanted finally to do what Reagan had only talked about. The moderates wanted to keep talking. "We've already given at the office," Pat Roberts told the *New York Times* in early 1995. "I don't know how much is enough." This was before Republicans had made any cuts at all.

It seemed unlikely, to say the least, that this battle would resolve itself in the $200 billion or so in annual reductions that would be necessary to balance the budget in seven years. Liberals waited in the wings, ready to denounce a farcical replay of Reagan's 1981 budget, which created the deficit by reducing taxes and increasing military spending without offsetting domestic cuts. Skepticism grew as the May 1 budget deadline came and went. But then, mirabile dictu, House and Senate Republicans actually produced balanced budget resolutions filled with proposals for specific cuts. This was a tribute to the energy of Kasich but even more to the shrewdness of Gingrich, who handed Kasich the reins. Gingrich seemed to have determined that a rerun of Reaganism was simply not among his available options. Some real cutting, and the political risk that accompanied it, was unavoidable. Thus round one went to the radicals, acting in concert with the closet libertarians.

In delivering this proposal and passing it with the loss of only a few Republican votes, Gingrich's conservatism proved itself to have more integrity than the Reaganite version. It paid a price, though. Almost immediately, Democrats began to score points with people who voted for smaller government but didn't want it to reduce anything specific—school lunches, or environmental spending, or college loans. In the fall of 1995 Democrats hit the jackpot, when Republicans spelled out a modest and entirely necessary reduction in the rate of growth in Medicare expenditures. Pressed by the need to find savings, Gingrich was forced to whack a middle-class constituency of people who vote, not those at the margins of society. His personal popularity, never very high, plummeted accordingly.

And that was just at the prospect of cuts. There is a huge distance between the promise to balance the budget at a slightly lower level of revenue, and the hundreds of billions in actual reductions that will be required to achieve it over the next seven years. Once the public actually begins to feel the effects of balancing the budget, pressure will build on the G.O.P. to modify its plan. Gingrich's task, in maintaining a majority and holding together a coalition to follow through, remains immense. Significant budget cuts—something Americans have never really experienced before—threaten Republicans from without and within. They give otherwise idea-starved Democrats something to bark about, and risk separating politically pragmatic moderates from the coalition. To avoid this, Republicans must turn to social issues. But this is hazardous. After welfare reform, which commands a strong conservative consensus, social issues divide rather than unite the G.O.P. Stress is bound to rise between libertarians and authoritarians, who suffer from a fundamental philosophical incompatibility on anything having to do with education, sexuality, or free expression. The same goes for absolutist positions on environmental and industrial deregulation, where Gingrich has had to steer away from his original "revolutionary" position to prevent defections. He understands that to prevent a crack-up, he must tacitly negate his negation of government. Pulling punches is a trick Gingrich may have learned from studying Reagan, who was a master of the art of calculated ineffectuality when it came to abortion. Reagan understood that on certain issues, a Republican leader must appease his party's extremists without allowing them to drag the party toward political suicide.

So far, Gingrich's marriage of contradictory philosophies has held up. But it cannot survive a real revolution. A government that is actually smaller in a meaningful way would mean things not yet contemplated even by the radicals—the removal of at least some of the major federal functions and responsibilities added since the New Deal, and the reduction of federal spending from its present level of 22 percent of GDP. One cannot categorically rule out Republicans' trying to get the government down to, say, the 18 percent where it stood before the Great Society. They have defied doubts about their seriousness of purpose before. But such a course does seem profoundly unlikely. To really shrink the federal government would alienate the middle-income voters who have been drawn away from the Democrats over the last thirty years.

A significantly smaller government, one the size we had during the Kennedy years, would allow for large, across-the-board tax cuts. It might boost the national rate of savings and investment, which would in turn foster additional economic growth. But it would also increase social misery. The unemployed and those in poorly compensated jobs would, under a true conservative regime, have to do without not just welfare and housing subsidies, Medicaid and food stamps, but fuel assistance, training programs, unemployment compensation, and the earned income tax credit. Though the radicals argue that charity is a substitute for government, there's little basis for believing private philanthropy will be able to do more than dull the pain. Charities mitigate suffering, but they cannot create jobs, which are what lift people out of poverty; only the private business sector and government can do that. And where would charities get the money to help millions of indigents? From government?

The boom in misery that would result from radically smaller government would mean political disaster for Gingrich. Thus, though the Speaker appears bolder than Reagan, his conundrum is the same. Selective inaction is the key to his party's retaining its hard-won viability. Gingrich has said, for instance, that changes in Social Security need to wait a decade. He has promised to step down as Speaker in eight years. This winking acknowledgment that the New Deal is untouchable keeps the moderates on board. Not saying he opposes touching Social Security holds open the hope of fundamental change and prevents libertarians from getting too upset. Gingrich names "big government" the enemy of civil society, of the free market, and of opportunity. He thrives on the resentment he helps to generate. But what he really offers is still an echo, not a choice. As he is unable to consummate his attack, his rhetoric grows increasingly baroque. He portrays the federal government as an external malevolent force. But he dares not strike at its heart, for fear of wounding himself. Our Republican is left huffing and puffing on a stationary bicycle, trying to convince himself and others that he's going somewhere. Or, to take another image, he is like a crazed used-car salesman, offering a damaged government at a slight discount. As we ponder our decision, he continues to scratch and kick it.

The Republican crack-up will occur in one of two ways. Sometime after the 1996 election, Gingrich—if he is still the Speaker—will face a decision: either he will proceed with a real revolution or he won't. If he tries to change the size and scope of the federal government by reversing the New Deal, he will surely fracture his coalition. Working people attracted to the G.O.P. in recent decades can be expected to turn away if Republicans repudiate rather than just trim the entitlements that underwrite middle-class security. If they take such action, moderates in Congress can be expected to break with their party and engender an effective if not an actual Democratic majority.

If, on the other hand, Gingrich decides faking it is the safer option, the gap between his words and his actions will grow unmanageable. Especially if Republicans capture the White House in 1996, he cannot continue to denounce the liberal welfare state without striking. If he does so, his party will once again be caught bluffing, talking about a revolution without storming the Bastille. Gingrich will be traduced, as Clinton was, for representing himself as one thing, then becoming another in office. If Gingrich cops out, he will lose the dedicated support of the freshmen as well as that of the closet libertarians. It is possible that both things will happen, as with Reagan. What Gingrich cannot do, and knows he cannot do, is reverse the New Deal and survive.

Liberals should be comforted, but only slightly. The moment of Republican crisis will not bring back faith in government by itself. It will only create an opportunity to do so. Unless liberals reassess and renew their own governing philosophy, the conservative crisis will avail them little; it will simply turn American politics into a standoff between two exhausted armies. For the Republican evasion is matched by a Democratic one, longer in the making and just as deeply ingrained.

Chapter Four

THE DEMOCRATIC CONFUSION

The worst enemy of true progress is the demagogue, or the visionary, who, in the name of progress, leads the people to make blunders such that in the resulting reaction they tend to distrust all progress. Distrust the demagogue and the mere visionary just as you distrust the hide-bound conservative.

— THEODORE ROOSEVELT, 1910

SHORTLY AFTER the 1994 election, as the Democratic president was changing his mind for the fourth or fifth time about how to respond to the Republican revolution, Jesse Jackson devastatingly remarked that when Clinton comes to a fork in the road he always chooses the fork. Striving to make everyone happy is, of course, an attribute of personality for Clinton. But it is not merely that. Clinton's ideological meandering reflects the condition of the Democratic Party itself. Various factions are urging it to go different ways. One would like to choose a path—but it's not clear that any of them lead to safety. In such a situation, striding in one clear direction may or may not help.

To understand how they landed in this predicament, one must consider how Democrats got to be the party of big government in the first place—how, with apologies again to Kipling, the donkey got its long ears. They weren't always that way. While Republicans were reversing their historical position to become the more government-averse of the two parties, Democrats were also switching positions. Their transformation, accomplished somewhat earlier, was from an antistatist liberalism to the activist, interventionist kind that has predominated in the twentieth century.

The old party of Thomas Jefferson and Andrew Jackson saw powerful government as a threat to its egalitarian ideals. Jacksonian Democrats thought a stronger federal government could lend advantage only to the rich and powerful; though the size of the federal government grew under his administration, Jackson bitterly opposed the Bank of the United States and other institutions that centralized power in Washington. His views continued to define the party until almost the end of the nineteenth century. It is no small irony, then, that the Democratic faithful who turn out for Jefferson–Jackson Day dinners are today excoriated by Republicans as champions of the leviathan. The ancestors Democrats still venerate were big government's original enemies.

Grover Cleveland, the only Democratic president who interrupted the long Republican hegemony after the Civil War, was the last of the old line. The 1892 platform on which he was elected sounded the tocsin as ever against the hazard of a presidential "monarchy." It deplored "the tendency to centralize all power at the Federal capital" as "a menace to the reserved rights of the States that strikes at the very roots of our Government under the Constitution as framed by the fathers of the Republic." Stirring words, but the philosophy of laissez-faire left Cleveland and the Democrats resourceless in answering the panic and depression of 1893. That crisis provided an opening for William Jennings Bryan, who supplanted Cleveland as the party's standard-bearer in 1896 by proposing aggressive remedies for hard times. Though Bryan never became president, and though the Democrats lost four consecutive elections with his help, the party would never again stand for smaller government or less intervention than the Republicans. After a hundred years, the Democrats traded in their belief in limited government for a commitment to federal activism, Hamiltonian means to Jeffersonian ends, in the familiar characterization. Their goal would still be a republic of equals, but now they would use the power of the national government to advance it.

This transformation was not simply the work of one demagogue named Bryan. It was wrought by the movement he represented. Populism first emerged in the late 1880s as an expression of the economic misery of midwestern farmers. What ailed them above all was deflation and the sinking prices of agricultural commodities. In answer to this, the populists proposed measures that would cause inflation, either a return to the free coinage of silver or the issuance of paper currency. Hence the now arcane lexicon of 1896: the Silver Republicans, who walked out of the monometalist G.O.P.; the Greenback Party, which advocated paper money; and the most famous convention speech in American history, Bryan's "Cross of Gold."

The populist movement transcended the currency issue and came to encompass a demand for intervention on behalf of urban and industrial workers as well. Populists asserted the need for government protection from the ravages of big business and monopoly. They also clamored for a variety of procedural reforms they thought would advance their cause and enshrine popular power in place of the moneyed interests: the direct election of senators; a one-term limit for presidents; the initiative and referendum; and the secret ballot.

Bryan stuck to a hands-off attitude when it came to foreign policy, giving rise to a strain of isolationism that still runs in his party. But in domestic and economic matters, he turned the ass into an ambitious beast. During the phase of Bryan's leadership, which stretched until 1912, the Democrats embellished their platform with protections for farmers and workers. "As labor creates the wealth of the country, we demand the passage of such laws as may be necessary to protect it in all its rights," asserted the party's 1896 credo. It spelled out these rights to include the eight-hour day, the progressive income tax instead of the tariff, antimonopoly law, and even public ownership of the means of communication and transportation. Under Bryan, Democrats also became the party of Prohibition.

But Bryan never got elected. The first Democratic president who stood for the new approach was Woodrow Wilson. Wilson looked at first like a reversion to the old liberal, Cleveland type of Democrat. In an earlier incarnation, he criticized the regulation of railways and corporations, denounced unions, and refused to share a platform with Bryan. But just as populism swept the nation in the 1890s, the Progressive movement overwhelmed it in the run-up to the election of 1912. Progressivism shared with populism an aversion to big business and especially the trusts, as they were known. It was likewise devoted to political reforms like the initiative and referendum, and was unequivocal in its advocacy of women's suffrage. But there were important differences too. Progressivism was more urban and less agrarian. In place of free silver, it substituted labor reform. And as expressed by Wilson, it urged upon government an obligation to break up monopoly in order to foster competition, not supplant it with public ownership or centralized direction, as many populists wished.

Wilson's first two years in office represent the fountainhead of modern, activist government. Though elected by a plurality in a three-way race, Wilson charged ahead. With control of both houses for the first time since 1896, the Democrats in 1913 and 1914 passed a raft of legislation intended to enhance competition, fracture trusts, and protect workers. Wilson called his program the New Freedom, describing it in strikingly radical language as freeing the country from its "masters . . . the combined capitalists and manufacturers of the United States." Most important to industrial workers were the creation of a Department of Labor, with the mandate to "foster, promote and develop the welfare of wage earners, to improve their working conditions, and to advance their opportunities for profitable employment," and the Clayton Act, which exempted unions from antitrust law. The list of Wilson's other accomplishments includes child-labor law, the eight-hour day for railway workers, improved conditions for sailors, banking reform, and the regulation of unfair business practices through the Federal Trade Commission. Wilson's first term also saw the advent of redistributionism in the form of the progressive income tax.

The end of World War I brought an economic downturn, and with it a powerful reaction against the Democrats that lasted through the 1920s. As the economy improved under Warren Harding, Republicans once again came to be seen as the guardians of national prosperity. Confronted with rejection, Democrats staged a partial retreat from Wilsonian progressivism. The party's 1924 candidate, John W. Davis, represented a half-step back in the direction of Cleveland; its platform of that year condemned the growth of bureaucracy and restored a states' rights plank Wilson had removed. Al Smith, who carried the standard in 1928, was slightly more Wilsonian in outlook, but like Davis failed to draw sharp distinctions between himself and the Republicans. After Smith's defeat, New York governor Franklin Roosevelt lamented the absence of "a progressive attack against the Coolidge-Hoover economic program."

The 1932 Democratic platform might have been viewed as another throwback to the days of Cleveland. A sober and responsible document, it called for balancing the federal budget by means of an "immediate and drastic reduction of governmental expenditures." Once elected, of course, Roosevelt did anything but. His reaction to the Great Depression was the antithesis not just of Hoover's helplessness but of Cleveland's passivity in 1893. The story of the New Deal doesn't need retelling here. What does bear remarking is that it was Roosevelt in 1932 who fixed the political labels that remain to this day. If Byran and Wilson changed the meaning of the term *Democrat,* FDR revised what it meant to be a liberal by applying that name to his own progressive program. Until Roosevelt, *liberal* meant what it meant in the nineteenth century: a belief in individual rights and laissez-faire. Hoover bitterly resented the usurpation of this term and for years fought unsuccessfully to reclaim it. It was Roosevelt too who tagged the Republicans with the label *conservative.* Eventually they quit struggling against that appellation, but in the 1930s the term conveyed even more opprobrium than the word *liberal* does today.

In political terms, the New Deal took the old members of the Democratic coalition—southern whites, urban Catholics, and union workers—and added new groups: blacks, Jews, and the poor in general. This became a durable majority of people who, even after the Depression, looked to the federal government for help with their problems. The party retained their loyalty even as they prospered. By 1952 registered Democrats outnumbered Republicans two to one. Harry Hopkins described the new liberal philosophy as "tax and tax, spend and spend, elect and elect," a formula that Republicans would later truncate and disparage to great effect. But the Roosevelt playbook was so successful that Democrats essentially followed it without revision for more than forty years. And even now that the New Deal model has fallen upon hard times, no clear alternative has emerged to replace Roosevelt's vision.

FDR's great dodge was his evasion of the race issue. Because of the entrenched power of the South in Congress and within the Democratic Party, he could do nothing but avoid it. Largely through force of personality, he managed to bring northern blacks into a coalition with southern racists and keep them there. But with Roosevelt's passing, the liberal demand for racial change rose and the issue came to threaten the Democratic majority. When Truman happened upon the presidency, he was known as a conservative and hence was greatly suspect among progressives and liberals. Those who considered themselves FDR's true heirs even contemplated jumping to the G.O.P., where they wouldn't have to kowtow to racists. Truman's order to desegregate the armed forces and the other pro–civil rights stands he adopted only partially appeased them. Meanwhile, these positions made southern conservatives wary of Truman as well. The New Deal coalition hung in an unstable equilibrium, liable to snap its left or right cable at any moment. Truman's attempt to balance these factions during his first term made him a figure of mockery and, according to the conventional wisdom, a highly unlikely prospect for reelection in 1948.

In the election of that year, both progressives and segregationists did abandon the party. The former supported the independent candidacy of former vice president and fellow traveler Henry Wallace. The latter endorsed Strom Thurmond, who ran on the "Dixiecrat" or states' rights ticket. Perhaps this dual rupture assured the nation as a whole that Truman was a centrist at heart. In any case, he beat Dewey by arguing forcefully for expanding the federal role in areas that had little to do with race. Truman proposed a plan of national health care insurance, paid for by payroll deductions, and a program of slum clearance. He demanded a massive federal housing program, aid to education, an expansion of Social Security, price and rent controls, and an increase in the minimum hourly wage. After the election, he called this package the Fair Deal. Much of it was rejected by Congress. But by 1952 Truman had delivered a list of important benefits to the aspiring middle class, including the G.I. Bill, Veterans Administration loans, loans for college students, and mortgages underwritten by the Federal Home Loan bank system. It was these works that prevented a permanent fracture in the Democratic coalition over race and transformed Truman's reputation from that of a parochial machine politician to that of liberal deity.

The next four elections can be seen as variations on the theme of balancing reciprocally antagonistic left and right flanks within the party. Adlai Stevenson, John F. Kennedy, and Lyndon B. Johnson all had enough conservatism in their backgrounds to reassure southern reactionaries and make progressives suspicious. Each tried to edge toward the latter without launching the former into orbit. In time, all three came to argue for substantial expansions of government power on the New Deal model. Stevenson, who according to legend was so fiscally austere that as governor of Illinois he had ordered the little flags on his limousine tied down so they wouldn't wear out so quickly, became a full-throated advocate of "human needs" and the champion of more equal distribution of the national abundance. His 1956 position papers detailed elaborate plans for federal action on health care, civil rights, public electric power, education, and aid to depressed areas.

Kennedy, who was chastised for having supported Joe McCarthy, emerged as the champion of various accretions to the federal role forestalled by Eisenhower: an expansion of public housing, aid to education, welfare, and unemployment benefits. If, following the advice of Arthur Schlesinger, Kennedy tried to· emphasize a "qualitative" rather than a "quantitative" liberalism, the redistributive school was back before long. It was Johnson who came forward with the most ambitious plan of all to complete and extend the New Deal—Medicare, Medicaid, and the War on Poverty.

LBJ's reelection in 1964, by the largest margin since FDR's in 1936, seemed a clear public mandate for this course. But soon the form of the expansion was pleasing neither faction. The New Left, which in the 1960s acted the part of the old Henry Wallace Progressives, abhorred Johnson's Vietnam War and considered his domestic programs half-measures. Segregationists were appalled by his conversion to the cause of civil rights. As in 1948, both factions split off. With challenges from Eugene McCarthy and George Wallace, and with the war growing more unpopular by the day, LBJ chose not to seek a second term.

Johnson's stand-in, Hubert Humphrey, sought desperately to hold the old New Deal majority together as Truman had. But 1968 was different from 1948 in two crucial respects. First, three decades after the New Deal there was no longer any plausible threat that Republicans would attempt to uproot it. Goldwater had taught them that lesson; Nixon knew better than to run against the legacy of FDR. Second, and perhaps more important, America in 1968 was still riding one of the most fantastic stretches of economic growth in the country's history. The middle class had become comfortable. On the basis of self-interest, fewer saw themselves benefiting from another round of intervention targeted at the have-nots. In this sense, New Deal liberalism can be seen as a victim of its own success. In sowing the seeds of a wider prosperity, it accidentally raised a crop of Republicans.

The Crisis Arrives

Humphrey's defeat inspired a peculiar sort of rethinking. The 1972 Democratic platform began with acknowledgments that the people felt "skeptical" and "cynical" about politics and government. Its answer, however, was, as Thomas Geoghegan wrote at the time, to "repackage the Great Society grocery list." In the words of the minority report of the Wallace faction, which again split off in 1972: "What this platform says is 'Government has failed—give us more government.'" After George McGovern's defeat the Democrats became self-conscious, dwelling endlessly on their own seeming inability to win presidential elections. A series of schemes for renovation emerged: the Scoop Jackson critique, which argued for a return to the Cold War internationalism of Roosevelt, Truman, and Kennedy and led to the creation of a group called the Coalition for a Democratic Majority; neoconservatism, which eventually gave up on the party as a vehicle for its ideas; and neoliberalism, a Democratic philosophy of reform government. There were those too who wanted the Democrats to stay the course, to remain the party of big, generous, and ever-expanding government.

But the rethinking was interrupted by the more impressive Republican catastrophe of Watergate. For the Democrats, Watergate was a curse disguised as a blessing. Just as they were beginning to take seriously their own intellectual and electoral difficulties, the problem was solved for them by a deus ex machina. Gary Hart, elected to the Senate from Colorado in 1974, was an exception among the huge class of liberal Democrats who swept into Congress on the Watergate tide. He was the only one who felt it necessary to openly question the old Roosevelt formula. Hart asserted the New Deal's "bankruptcy" and promised more prudent fiscal management.

The following election year, 1976, was the first in which the Democrats fielded a candidate who stood somewhat outside the New Deal–Great Society tradition. Jimmy Carter didn't reject the New Deal, or the party's base. Yet, under the tutelage of Pat Caddell, he tried to widen a shrinking coalition by adding economic conservatives skeptical of ever-expanding federal government. Carter ran against Washington and used *bureaucrat* as a term of abuse. One of his few specific campaign promises was to cut the federal bureaucracy from 1,900 agencies to 200, as he had slimmed Georgia's from 300 to 22, though he remained vague about how he planned to do this.

Carter outraged liberals. It wasn't that he wanted to cut spending; he just proposed raising it by a smaller amount than advocates for labor and minority groups insisted. In resisting interest-group demands, Carter antagonized the congressional wing of his own party and provoked a primary challenge from Ted Kennedy in 1980. Kennedy supported gasoline rationing and a freeze on wages and profits as an answer to inflation. He opposed any cuts in social programs. In a powerful convention speech that year, he urged his party not to let "the great purposes of the Democratic Party become the bygone passages of history." The real effect of the Kennedy challenge was to pull the incumbent to the left; in 1980 Carter ran as a Democratic traditionalist. He had outgrown his dislike of bureaucrats and the ways of Washington.

After Carter's defeat in 1980, the crisis of liberalism was evident to all. Democrats had lost three out of four presidential elections and won the remaining one only with the help of the worst scandal in American history. Their response was to found think tanks and hold seminars in hopes of finding their way back to victory. Opinion diverged fundamentally on the question of whether the party needed to change its basic governing philosophy. Carter, by venturing one alternative and then retreating, complicated the question. The paleoliberals, as the *New Republic* took to calling them, argued that the problem wasn't New Deal liberalism but rather Carter's ambivalence about it. Redistribution, they believed, was by definition smart politics. On the other hand the neoliberals (a term coined by Charles Peters of the *Washington Monthly*) contended that Carter had been insufficiently devoted to change. They saw a problem with the methodology of liberalism. Democrats could continue to pursue their old goal of a more egalitarian society, neoliberals argued, but should be more pragmatic about it, eschewing big bureaucracies and the interest groups that demanded ever more of them.

What emerged within the party was a version of the old left-right split. The 1984 primary came down to a fight between Gary Hart and Walter Mondale. Hart argued that "the Democratic Party must govern well, but it must not be the party of government." Mondale responded by denying there was a problem. He rallied the interest groups that made up the party's base and announced in advance that a tax hike would be necessary to undo the Reagan deficit while avoiding cuts in social programs. But tax and tax, spend and spend, no longer resulted in elect and elect. During the campaign, Reagan said he planned to scare people on Halloween by dressing up as Mondale's tax program. In 1984 the Democrats ran as the old party of big government and lost forty-nine states.

The old liberals argued that their cause had been undermined by Mondale's drab personality and his eat-your-spinach approach to politics. But they had had their chance. After Mondale's defeat, the search for alternatives began in earnest. Following the election, a congressional group called the Democratic Leadership Council constituted itself as the conservative wing of the Democratic Party. The DLC, principally composed of southerners, argued that more "big government" was not the answer to society's problems. It looked like this faction might have its chance in 1988. But then the leading DLC candidate, Gary Hart, withdrew because of a sex scandal, surrendering the field to Michael Dukakis. Like Carter, Dukakis blurred the issue of what the Democrats' governing philosophy should be. He eschewed class-based politics and promised greater efficiency and procedural reform. But he had no distinctive agenda of his own. Dukakis contended that the issue was "competence" not "ideology," which was a way of saying he was neither for more big government nor against it. In 1988 the Democrats ran as the party of soulless better government and got creamed again.

A Democratic Anatomy

How can the Democrats be the party of government—the party of Wilson, FDR, and Truman (if not of Johnson)—in an age when government is discredited and disliked? And if they are something other than advocates of activist government, what defines them as Democrats?

The answer to these questions sorts out the party today. Just as Republicans divide into a libertarian avant-garde and a reactionary rump, the Democrats can be anatomized according to their beliefs about government. Like the Republicans, they consist of a relatively small revisionist intelligentsia that wields an influence disproportionate to its size, and a more conventionally minded mass. To oversimplify a bit, the elite consists of those who call themselves New Democrats and want to revise the New Deal–Great Society model. The rank and file is made up of old liberals who, in varying degrees, still cling to it.

When the Democratic Leadership Council was organized in 1985 its core was composed of conservative southern and western legislators; the best known were Sam Nunn of Georgia and Chuck Robb of Virginia. The DLC's original objection to Democratic orthodoxy was twofold. The exodus of middle-class voters from the party, the group's leaders contended, was explained by its pattern of domination by liberal interest groups. Kissing up to special interests was self-defeating, they argued, since it served to alienate the country's massive middle class. The other key issue was defense and foreign policy, where they rejected their party's post-Vietnam isolationism. The DLCers were hawks, alumni of the Scoop Jackson wing and the Coalition for a Democratic Majority. Many of them voted with the Reagan administration in support of military aid to the Nicaraguan contras. At its 1991 convention the DLC passed a controversial resolution supporting American involvement in the Gulf War, which was a minority position within the party as a whole.

Since the end of the Cold War foreign policy has diminished in political significance and the DLC has concentrated on developing its critique of domestic liberalism. The New Democrats, as they took to calling themselves in the early nineties, believe that liberal positions on social issues like busing and crime combined with the party's dovishness on foreign policy to destroy its natural majority at the presidential level. As the middle class grew and the unionized working class shrank, government intervention became increasingly irrelevant to most people. Al From, who has been the president of the DLC since its inception, argues that today most people think of themselves as taxpayers rather than as beneficiaries of government programs.

The DLC answer to the loss of the middle class is to focus on its problems rather than those of the poor. Like Stanley Greenberg, the New Democrats posit a strategy for recovering the lost votes of the angry white suburbanites of Macomb County. To do this, they believe Democrats must rebuff the excessive demands of special-interest and pressure groups like the AFL-CIO, the Rainbow Coalition, the National Organization for Women, and the ACLU. The DLC made clear how this would work by pointedly uninviting Jesse Jackson to its own 1991 convention. New Democrats believe that the interest groups have spurred the creation of social programs that demand too little of their beneficiaries and fail to promote responsible behavior. New Democrats want a government that learns from the private sector, one that is more flexible and businesslike and that restores a moral dimension to public policy. Since 1989 the development of detailed proposals embodying these ideas has been the work of the Progressive Policy Institute (PPI), an affiliated think tank.

As chairman of the DLC in 1990 and 1991, Bill Clinton helped elaborate this critique. "The working people and small-business people that used to vote for us don't anymore in a lot of tough elections because they have become convinced that the Democrats won't stand up for American interests abroad . . . [and] will tax the middle class to give it to the poor with no strings attached," Clinton told a group of Louisiana Democrats in 1991. In response to this misguided tendency, Clinton declared solidarity during his presidential campaign with "the forgotten middle class." He made strenuous efforts to show that he was not a tool of the old interest groups, publicly provoking both Jesse Jackson and the AFL-CIO. He chastised "the brain-dead policies of left and right" and talked about welfare as a failed government program. His "New Covenant" (a phrase attributed to PPI president Will Marshall) stressed the reciprocal obligations of citizenship, not just the benefits offered by government. That year, the party's luck finally changed. In 1992 the Democrats ran as the party of reform government attuned to the nation's moral values, and won.

Suddenly the New Democrats were inside the city gates, or so it seemed. The DLC-PPI published its Mandate for Change, modeled on Mandate for Leadership, the influential Heritage Foundation report of 1980. But though they had contributed to Clinton's victory, the New Democrats clearly had an ongoing job of persuasion on their hands. When appointments were made, there were only a few New Democrats in the top ranks. The president did not immediately pursue welfare reform, the issue that the DLC considered both a moral imperative and the key to solidifying his middle-class support. Instead, he focused his attention on creating a new federal entitlement to health care. Though he did propose deficit reduction, which the New Democrats lauded, and advanced a national service program, which was a pet cause of theirs, they found Clinton's efforts wanting. Several DLC members in Congress were soon in open conflict with the administration over the size of Clinton's spending cuts and his proposal for an increase in the gas tax.

The group as a whole was torn between working from inside to try to influence the president and writing him off as a hopeless sellout. Al From and Clinton were like a couple that fights in public; their constant breaking up and getting back together began to look ridiculous. After Democrats lost control of Congress in 1994, DLC leaders were disenchanted enough to talk openly about supporting a third-party candidate in 1996 or backing a primary challenge to Clinton. But as the president reached again for the center in the spring of 1995, they quieted their complaints. Instead, it was now the old Democrats who began to lose patience with Clinton. Soon the positions were reversed again. Given the antagonism between the DLC and the traditionalist wing of the party, and Clinton's need to appease both sides, this dance is likely to continue for as long as he remains president. What pleases the majority of congressional Democrats by definition annoys the DLC.

Why has Clinton been so halfhearted about the DLC and its ideas? It may be because, while rightly dissatisfied with paleoliberalism, the New Democrats haven't come up with a fully plausible alternative plan for recapturing Democratic voters gone astray. The most influential New Democratic idea—and perhaps the only widely read New Democratic book—is *Reinventing Government,* published in 1992 by PPI fellow David Osborne and Ted Gaebler, the former city manager of Visalia, California. *Reinventing Government* is a study of public-sector innovation, particularly at the state and local level, where it offers heroic anecdotes of nonbureaucratic thinking, and attempts to delineate the principles of what the authors call "entrepreneurial government."

Osborne and Gaebler are heavily influenced by management philosophy, particularly such authors as Peter Drucker, Thomas Peters (who wrote *In Search of Excellence*), and W. Edwards Deming, the father of "total quality management." The authors distill these ideas into easy axioms. Government should "steer" and not "row"; "empower," not "serve"; fund "outcomes" rather than "inputs"; earn rather than spend; prevent rather than cure. Osborne and Gaebler propose these concepts as an alternative both to the New Deal–Great Society model of expanding bureaucratic government and the Goldwater-Reagan model of shrinking it. "The central failure of government today is one of means, not ends," they write. "We do not need more government or less government, we need better government. To be more precise we need better governance."

Clinton embraced this idea at the outset of his presidency; Osborne's book was the inspiration behind the National Performance Review, a.k.a. reinventing government, or Rego as it was known, a project directed by Vice President Al Gore. New Democrats were disappointed (their permanent condition) that Clinton did not devote himself more wholeheartedly to it. And indeed, there was little downside for the president in drawing attention to efforts to eliminate redundancies and absurdities in Washington. Gore's staff developed many useful ideas for making bureaucracy more efficient by reducing field offices, consolidating duplicative efforts, and even terminating a few obsolete programs.

Rego brought significant, practical reforms that were politically advantageous as well. Government waste is a universal bogeyman; Gore's project was the first time an administration tried to address it in a systematic and serious way. Broadly conceived, reinvention is a notion that can help to revive the Democrats. It gives them a handle for the ongoing process of asking basic questions about what government should and shouldn't do. But at its heart, the Clinton-Gore effort had a severe conceptual flaw. "Today, the central issue we face is not *what* government does, but *how* it works," asserted the introduction to the first Rego report, echoing Osborne and Gaebler. Thus from the start, Rego declared its intention not to ask fundamental questions about government's responsibilities. It leapfrogged issues of what government should do in favor of figuring out how government can do everything it now does more efficiently. Nowhere did its applica-

tion of market principles suggest anything so bold as getting the
Commerce Department out of the business of providing subsidies
to profit-making enterprises or means-testing entitlements.

With this constricted vision, Rego became a victim of the management hype that dominates Osborne's book; Gore's report prat-
tles endlessly about "putting customers first," the need to "make the
federal government customer-friendly" and "measure our success by customer satisfaction." This is a dismal and demeaning view
of government. The subjects of the United States are citizens in a
democracy, not customers in a Wal-Mart. Certain functions—the
post office, the motor vehicle department—can benefit from a
more corporate approach. But viewing government as a whole in
this way breeds a what's-in-it-for-me mentality that lies at the
heart of the problem.

Government has a problem of *what* as well as one of *how*. Is it
up to government to "steer" health care to everyone? Should it
provide housing for the poor? Should it offer welfare? At a time
when consensus on such issues no longer exists, the question of
whether such goals are even valid must precede analysis of the
best way to carry them into practice. After the 1994 election,
Clinton thought a beefed-up Rego might help him provide an
answer to the Republicans and phase two of the project did begin
to ask, in a broader way, what government should and shouldn't
be doing in the first place. But still Rego tended to evade difficult
choices and thereby fall short of its potential.

It would be unfair to dismiss the DLC as merely the cult of the
efficiency expert. New Democrats don't want to be seen as heartless technocrats or Dukakisoids and do strive for a moral
approach to politics. They also understand how government can
really save money. PPI has been the principal group pointing out
that the middle class gets all sorts of hidden benefits—Social
Security beyond what is deserved or needed, all manner of subsidies, and tax benefits like the home mortgage interest deduction
and deductible health insurance. Means testing these programs
has been the group's boldest and best suggestion. But such ideas

also put the DLC in the paradoxical position of striving to win back the affection of the middle class while pushing it away from the government teat. The DLC slogan might be: "Come home to the Democrats—we'll cut you off."

There is a way to resolve this tension, which is to appeal to a broader definition of self-interest. The DLC's solution, however, has usually been to create common enemies for the middle class. The DLC has gone out of its way to repulse anyone whose Democratic identity relates to membership in an interest group. The plight of African-Americans must remain central to anything that pretends to call itself liberalism. The DLC, however, has done all it can to move the party away from acting to help blacks. It supports "tough" welfare reform that would cut off those unwilling to work, but it has no plausible scenario for where jobs for those on the dole would come from. It is too allergic to old liberal solutions to propose a sensible public employment program, clinging instead to the faint hope that welfare mothers will find work in the private sector. Abandoning race-based affirmative action, which Will Marshall of PPI has advocated, would give up on one of the few efforts that tangibly helps blacks.

Politically, the DLC resembles other intellectual movements; like libertarians and neoconservatives, the New Democrats began without a constituency and have failed to develop one. Theirs remains a philosophy without a following. In the 1994 election the ranks of the New Democrats in Congress were not just thinned but virtually obliterated. The movement was left without a single visible leader in the House and, with Sam Nunn retiring, only a few in the Senate. As Al From has pointed out, those who lost represented districts that were only marginally Democratic—it's unlikely paleoliberals would have done better. Still, it's hard to say your plan is working when everyone who tries it loses.

Despite its limitations, the DLC has at least been trying to develop new ideas for the party. To hear some fellow Democrats tell it, you'd think it was an enemy organization. Since the formation of the DLC, the group has been regarded with open hostility by party traditionalists. One of the most persistent critics is Jesse Jackson, who suggests that the initials *DLC* actually stand for Democrats of the Leisure Class. Robert Kuttner, a liberal economic journalist, writes that the DLC represents "abandoning the party's progressive message" in favor of capitulation to its old southern racist wing. Mario Cuomo has scorned it for "confessing to sins we never committed." Barney Frank, the Massachusetts congressman, says "the notion of being rescued by the right wing of the DLC is like being on the *Lusitania* and being told the *Titanic* has been sent to rescue you."

The harshness of such accusations—especially the unwarranted charge of racism—bespeaks a deep anxiety on the part of paleoliberals. To them, New Democrats threaten the party's essence, though they do not agree among themselves whether that essence is racial justice, the expansion of universal benefits, or populist class warfare. In pointing out that the old-time religion gets fewer and fewer Democrats elected, the DLC raises a problem many old Democrats simply find too painful to discuss. By denouncing the DLC, party traditionalists manifest the classic urge to shoot the messenger.

What, then, do paleoliberals think is to be done? There are degrees of unenlightenment, ranging from those who deny that Democrats have a problem, political or substantive, to those who admit one but propose an inadequate remedy. But the most common alternatives—economic populism, economic nationalism, and a stand-pat approach that might be called reactionary liberalism—are of a piece. Though they are separate strains, they overlap in their resistance to change in the party's values, again variously defined. All want to make sure that Democrats don't break with their old pursuit of economic equality, the Jefferson–Jackson–New Deal–Fair Deal–Great Society tradition. Their favorite adage is Harry Truman's: "When the voters have a choice between a Republican and a Republican, they'll pick the Republican every time." Their reigning cliché is: "America doesn't need two Republican Parties."

The group with the greatest influence on the Clinton presidency has been the economic populists. Call this the Roseanne faction. Economic populists argue that the fundamental problem of the Democrats is that they have abandoned their working-class supporters—people like the characters on *Roseanne* who struggle to raise a family on two salaries, where one used to serve. Economic populists argue that in order to reclaim this vote, Democrats must adopt an explicitly redistributive strategy: soak the rich, lower taxes for workers, and create new universal benefits to help those struggling to make it. The cure for the Democrats, according to Kuttner, is returning to a politics explicitly aimed at the "working class," one that articulates "the economic self-interest of voters who live paycheck to paycheck and who are vulnerable to the uncertainties of the market economy."

Why did Democrats stop speaking for Roseanne? Economic populists give two reasons. The first is that the party of the New Deal got distracted by cultural and social issues in the sixties and seventies—principally race, feminism, and the Vietnam War. These were the preoccupations of the elite, not the rank and file (though economic populists often contradict themselves on this point by accusing the New Democratic elite of race baiting). The second reason is the structure of the political system. Campaign finance reform, a well-intentioned liberal effort, inadvertently exacerbated the problem by making Democrats beholden to business interests with PAC money to donate. In his book *The Life of the Party,* Kuttner names Tony Coelho, the former head of the Democratic Congressional Campaign Committee, as the personification of the problem. Coelho raised millions from corporations, making his party competitive with the well-lubricated Republican political machine of the Reagan years. But this was a Faustian bargain, which led the Democrats away from their people.

There is a slightly obsessive quality to the worldview of economic populism; all Democratic victories are attributed to the adoption of its message, all losses to the neglect of it. Walter Mondale's fatal mistake in 1984, Kuttner writes, was appearing as a

"Democratic Hoover" by calling for all-around austerity. Had he threatened to tax the wealthy beneficiaries of Reaganism instead, everything would have been hunky-dory. Again according to Kuttner, Democrats recaptured the Senate in 1986 on the basis of populist victories in several states; Jesse Jackson had a "surprising success" with white voters in the Michigan primaries in 1988; with a dab more populism, Dukakis could have been president. Economic populists are forever making the point that when Dukakis ventured a bit of Robin Hood rhetoric, briefly and late in the campaign, his popularity surged, only to falter when he dropped it. "Only when Dukakis began emphasizing traditional Democratic stands on the issues very late in the campaign did he begin to win back lost ground," notes Barney Frank, picking up where Kuttner leaves off.

Frank's 1992 book *Speaking Frankly: What's Wrong with the Democrats and How to Fix It* proposes a variant on straight economic populism. Like Kuttner, Frank faults the diversions of cultural politics for the decline of the party. He shares the belief that redistributive economic and social programs are the way to restored vigor. But Frank doesn't think the legacy of the New Left will be so easily overcome; the residue of the 1960s is that a majority of Americans still view the Democrats as unpatriotic. The voter Frank hopes to recapture is less Roseanne than Archie Bunker. To get that vote back, he argues, the party must stop pandering to its own left wing. Democrats can recapture the center by avowing their support for the military (while still advocating massive cuts in defense spending) and excoriating crime and criminals. In this effort at "inoculation," Frank mimics the view of the DLC. But for him, these changes do not imply a change in basic orientation. Rather, they are painless concessions that will allow Democrats to cash in their natural advantage as the party of programs and spending. As Frank put it in a 1990 *Harper's* Forum, referring to the Republicans: "I say we tie them on values, move on to programs, and beat 'em."

There was a strong element of populist strategy in Bill Clinton's 1992 campaign. Clinton distanced himself from the Democratic left on the use of military force, crime, and race, then punished George Bush with a class-based economic assault. Clinton took this tack on the counsel of his advisers James Carville and George Stephanopoulos and his pollster Stanley Greenberg. Greenberg provided the theory; on the basis of his work in Macomb, he recommended a further refinement of economic populism. His scheme was not to pit poor against rich but rather to side with a broad and intentionally ill-defined middle— Roseanne, Archie Bunker, and the regulars at Cheers too. Disagreeing with Kuttner, Greenberg contended that the party's class base was no longer a quasiproletariat but rather a suburbanized middle class frightened by the prospect of downward mobility. His view was that Clinton should declare solidarity with these people and stoke their anger at the narrow group that benefited unfairly from twelve years of Republican economics.

Like the New Democrats, economic populists can claim some share of the credit for Clinton's victory. And, likewise, they were disappointed by his performance in office. From the outset, populists criticized Clinton's unwillingness to offend Wall Street and were upset that his economic plan was a program of incremental change that emphasized deficit reduction. Populists also wanted Clinton to market his health care proposal as a crusade against the big interests—greedy insurance and pharmaceutical companies. After the 1994 debacle, they called for him to emulate Truman by assailing the Republican Congress as "gluttons of privilege." They succeeded briefly, by getting Clinton to renew his old call for a middle-class tax cut, which in a bit of grandiose newspeak he called a "middle-class Bill of Rights." But the tactic failed to register with the electorate and was soon returned to a back burner. Early in 1995 Clinton's populist advisers were widely reported to be out of favor.

The most familiar argument against economic populism is that it whips up invidious resentments that are counterproductive. Americans have an instinctive aversion to class-based politics, we are reminded. This is a nation that cherishes its ideal of social mobility, where classes are not fixed and eternal. Lower-class Americans hope to become middle class; the middle dreams of being rich. One should be a bit skeptical of this bromide. There are plenty of have-nots who would love to stick it to the haves—whether it improves their own station or not.

Given the right circumstances, economic populism can work as an electoral strategy. In 1992 after a long recession and twelve years of Republican administrations, the message had considerable salience. But such conditions are rare, and Democrats had better hope they stay that way. Economic populism is a good strategy for an opposition party in hard times, but no strategy at all for a party in power or for a period of growth, even if middle-class incomes are lagging behind. So long as prosperity is on the rise, Republicans can champion it as they did so successfully in the 1920s and at the presidential level in the 1950s and the 1980s. Even in periods of slower growth, economic progress erodes the material basis for such a pitch. As Bruce Babbitt once said, the problem with us-against-them politics is that there are not enough us and too many them. Clinton, after all, won only 43 percent of the vote under the propitious circumstances of 1992. Without Ross Perot, he might not have made it.

But even if economic populism were workable as a political strategy, it's not a practicable governing one, as Clinton discovered. As Mickey Kaus argues in his book *The End of Equality,* even steeply progressive taxes won't do much to reverse the long-term trend toward greater income inequality. That process is being driven by vast tectonic changes in the global economy. Thus "money liberals," as Kaus calls them, can't really deliver on their promises to the working class. A more progressive distribution of the tax burden may make sense. But, as Clinton learned after attempting it in 1993, redistribution has little effect on the underlying dynamic that is making the poor poorer and rich richer. The substantive problem with economic populism is that no one knows how to translate it into policies that will produce the desired result.

Like the populists, economic nationalists favor more redistribution. But nationalists think straightforward populism, with its emphasis on fairer taxation, doesn't go far enough. They demand meatier stuff. If populism appeals to the Roseanne vote, economic nationalism shares the worldview of the Japanophobic thriller *Rising Sun:* we are being bought out by ruthless foreigners. Falling wages and growing inequality are not the fault of a morally neutral, information-age economy, but rather of an external threat to the United States, which nationalists portray in stark martial language. It is a "real and present danger," an "invasion," and an issue of "security." Where economic populists style themselves after the Progressives, who wanted to break up concentrations of economic power for the benefit of the consumer, nationalists hark back to Bryan's populism. They are hostile to "elites" and "experts" and see themselves as champions of the toiling and forgotten.

Where economic populists focus on taxes, nationalists care about trade. Economic nationalism was born in the early 1980s, when politicians and journalists began to draw a connection between America's industrial decline and the growth of foreign (principally Japanese) competition. Richard Gephardt made unfair imports the theme of his presidential campaign in 1988. He claimed a Hyundai would cost $40,000 with all of the tariffs South Koreans put on American cars entering their own market. The NAFTA debate provided a better handle for the issue. Jeff Faux of the Economic Policy Institute, an economic nationalist think tank, decried Bush's negotiation of the treaty and in 1991 urged Democratic candidates to oppose its ratification. Faux argues that American laborers cannot compete with low-wage workers in Latin America and Asia and shouldn't have to try.

Like the populists, nationalists need to explain why the Democratic Party has failed to listen to their good advice. The reason, they argue, is political corruption, specifically influence peddling; foreigners own Washington. By acquiring the services of high-priced revolving-door lobbyists, they prevent America from pursuing its own economic interest. This is the case Martin and Susan Tolchin make in their book *The Selling of America* and Pat Choate makes in *Agents of Influence,* which documents efforts by

Japanese firms to acquire clout in Washington. There's even a watch group that focuses on this issue: the Center for Public Integrity, which tries to expose links between revolving-door lobbying and the free-trade policies pursued by Democratic and Republican administrations alike.

Like the New Democrats and economic populists, nationalists have influenced Bill Clinton. Faux was a peripheral adviser in 1992; a more influential one was Derek Shearer, a Friend of Bill's who served briefly at the commerce department. Nationalists saw an ally as well in Laura Tyson, an economist who argued for a policy of "managed trade" before she joined the administration. Robert Reich too, in his book *The Work of Nations,* called for a "positive" version of economic nationalism to counter the rising inequality he blamed in part on global competition. But nationalists were also disappointed with Clinton, more so than even the populists and the New Democrats. Their disenchantment started even before he was elected, when Clinton committed himself to support for NAFTA and free trade.

After that decision, nationalists moved increasingly to support Ross Perot. Perot did what nationalists have long recommended: he blamed America's problems on international laissez-faire. Perot articulated the theme with the folksy flair it seemed to demand; NAFTA, he famously quipped, would create a "giant sucking sound" along the U.S.-Mexican border as companies and jobs went south to take advantage of dollar-an-hour labor. Perot also connected lobbying and campaign finance to the problem, making them into potent issues for the first time.

Nationalists point to Perot's relative success in 1992 as evidence of their own potential. Though they remain tempted by a third-party alternative, most still see their future tied to that of the Democratic Party. They argue that Democrats must recapture the Perot voters, a group they view as more or less synonymous with the Reagan Democrats or Stanley Greenberg's Macombians, through the provision of red meat. "An enemy must be found against whom public support—and through that, congressional support—can be rallied," writes Ruy Teixeira, a

144 • IN DEFENSE OF GOVERNMENT

sociologist who works for the Economic Policy Institute. As scapegoat he nominates "recalcitrant sections of the business community as well as foreign economic powers whose successes appear to be threatening U.S. jobs and wages."

Note the use of the term *appear* in that passage. A worrisome trait of economic nationalists is their inability to distinguish strategy from reality. It is unclear whether Teixeira actually believes foreign economic powers are to blame for declining wages, or whether he simply needs a scourge to whip up anger. It appears to be the latter. Economic nationalists think Democrats must fight fire with fire, answering the cynicism of the Republicans with diabolical gambits of their own.

Nationalists justify such demagoguery by the need to build support for expensive, aggressive programs to raise the incomes of workers—the positive side of their approach. "The obvious solution to the political problem for the Democrats posed by the Perot voters is therefore to fix these economic problems without doing anything unusual in the way of government activism," writes Teixeira. That's like saying the obvious solution to the problem of global warming is to lower the earth's ambient temperature a few degrees without trying anything unusual in the way of scientific experimentation. Fixing the economic problems that distress Teixeira would amount to something not just unusual in the way of government activism, but unprecedented and perhaps impossible. The fight against income inequality today is at the stage of the War on Poverty in 1965. We barely understand the problem, and the enemy is even more protean. The same wishful thinking underlies the nationalist attack on foreign lobbying. Influence peddling distorts the democratic process to the advantage of moneyed interests, to be sure, but the foreign aspect of it is not the essence of its harm. Closing the revolving door may help reduce the deficit, as the power of special pleaders to garner tax breaks and subsidies diminishes, but it will not do much to help beleaguered industrial workers.

As a political strategy, economic nationalism has the potential to be effective with that segment of the old Democratic base that is suffering most severely from the shift to a postindustrial, global economy. It's a great pitch for winning the Michigan primary. But it is hard to make it out as a basis for drawing together a durable majority. Protectionism is a backward-looking idea, a point Al Gore articulated well in the *Larry King Live* NAFTA debate in which he trounced Perot. Though they might temporarily improve income equality, trade barriers would hamper overall prosperity to a far greater degree. Pursued as policy, protectionism would produce a nation worse off than under a regime of free trade. This urge to spread the misery characterizes other economic nationalist policies as well. For example, nationalists are constantly prodding the Federal Reserve to cut interest rates, to stimulate growth and employment. Though this risks bringing back inflation, nationalists follow the nineteenth-century populists in believing that inflation serves a useful redistributive function. It does redistribute, but at a cost of instability and constricted growth for the country as a whole.

But the worst of economic nationalism is the bigotry that lies just below its surface. It is an ideology that tends toward isolationism and xenophobia, a point underscored by the odd left-right, post–Cold War convergence of the *Nation* and Pat Buchanan on economic issues. You never hear economic nationalists railing about Dutch investment in America or the unfair trade practices of the Irish. The barbaric Chinese, the automaton-like Japanese, and the barefoot Mexicans are much more inviting targets. If economic populism is a strategy for hard times, economic nationalism is a strategy for catastrophic ones, in which the public turns to irrational scapegoating of foreigners, minorities, and immigrants. Such resentments are powerful, to be sure, but succeeding on such a basis would be a greater tragedy for the Democrats than honorable defeat.

Most leaders in the party, while intrigued by the populist and nationalist critiques, have not adopted either. Rather, they simply defend the Democratic status quo. It is perhaps unsurprising that the party's congressional leaders argued against reform before the 1994 election when, whatever their failures at the presidential level, they retained a solid hold on both houses of Congress.

What is amazing is that they have resisted reevaluation since being tossed out. In the face of a massive repudiation of the Clinton plan, many congressional Democrats continue to argue not just for health care reform but for a single-payer system. In the face of an overwhelming national demand for balancing the budget, they continue to dodge the issue. As ever, the only substantial budget cuts any of them support are in defense.

Their view is reactionary for the same reason that Herbert Hoover was reactionary. Faced with the Great Depression, a problem for which his ideology did not provide an answer, Hoover simply reasserted his beliefs. Faced with the loss of faith in government solutions, and a dynamic if flawed response from the G.O.P., reactionary liberals respond by defending government as it is. If they have adjusted at all, it has been at the level of rhetoric.

The paradigmatic reactionary liberal is Mario Cuomo. In the 1980s Cuomo often explained his theory of government as follows: "Of course we should have only the government we need. But we must insist on *all* the government we need." During the 1994 election, he tellingly adjusted the emphasis: "You should have all the government you need. But you should have *only* the government you need." In practice, this always meant the same thing: all the government he could get. In *Reason to Believe,* a book he published in 1995, Cuomo answers his defeat with an affirmation of faith. The voters of New York threw him out for giving them too much ineffective government at too high a cost. But to Cuomo, the horizon of government is still limitless; he briefly considers the notion that liberals need to rethink, then dismisses it.

When Gingrich attacks Democrats as defenders of a failed welfare state, he strikes a chord because Cuomo and his allies are at least defenders of a deeply flawed welfare system. Democrats are right to take credit for such successful programs as Head Start, food stamps, and the earned income tax credit. But in response to overwhelming evidence that a monthly AFDC check traps an underclass in poverty, they have failed to offer any plausible alternative. In response to public housing projects unfit for human habitation, they have tried to shore them up with more money. Democrats passed the law that forbids HUD from tearing down projects unless it can replace units on a one-for-one basis. In practice, this has meant pouring billions into hopeless sinkholes. In answer to the uncontrolled growth in the cost of Medicare, reactionary liberals have opposed any changes in the system. Theirs is a political Luddism. Reactionary liberalism corresponds to pseudolibertarianism on the right because it ignores government's failures, just as most Republicans close their eyes to its successes.

In trying to enhance the scope of government in a period of growing disaffection with it, reactionary liberalism has increasingly violated its own democratic principles. Faced with an electorate that resists additional public-sector growth, it has expanded the government by, as Malcolm X would say, any means necessary. Few things created so much ill will on the part of governors and state-level officials as Henry Waxman's efforts as chairman of the House health care subcommittee. In the 1980s and early 1990s, Waxman was constantly adding new requirements to the Medicaid program, the cost of which was foisted onto state governments with an inadequate federal supplement. These mandates were really an attempt to achieve national health insurance without winning a vote in favor of it. If the electorate said it didn't want to pay another dollar in taxes in exchange for another dollar in public goods, Democrats figured they could either make the private sector spend the dollar or spend it anyway and get the public to pay later.

With the loss of congressional power, however, there are no more avenues of expansion open to the Democrats. Thus reactionary liberals have returned to the strategy they pursued during the Reagan years: to portray Republicans as biased in favor of the rich and heartless in their desire to take benefits away from the vulnerable. After the 1994 election, reactionary liberals first erected pickets around the school lunch program. Thomas Daschle and Richard Gephardt's response to Gingrich's prime-time address to the nation at the end of the first hundred days of the 104th Congress was broadcast from an elementary school classroom in Arlington, Virginia. "Next year, there are children here who won't have school lunches," Gephardt proclaimed. "The Republicans cut them to pay for tax breaks for the wealthiest Americans." Once Republicans proposed a balanced budget, reactionary liberals took the offensive against cuts that would affect middle-class beneficiaries, Medicare, and student loans, linking them to tax cuts that would benefit "the privileged few."

Democrats were so pleased to be finally scoring points that they failed to notice how unsustainable their position was. If not college loans and Medicare (which go to relatively well off families as well as the poor), then what should be cut to balance the budget? They wouldn't discuss tax increases to solve the problem either. Reactionary liberal Democrats don't argue that big deficits are okay; they just shirk any rational approach to drawing them down. They spent most of 1995 taking potshots at Gingrich, seemingly untroubled that they have neither a substantive economic strategy nor any long-range political one.

THIS TAXONOMY neglects only one significant strategy of revival: communitarianism. If economic populism is the world according to *Roseanne* and economic nationalism is *Rising Sun,* communitarianism sees the world along the lines of *The Andy Griffith Show* and *Leave It to Beaver.* Communitarians long for a smaller world, where everyone knows everyone else, families are stable and traditional, cooperation and friendliness are the rule, and moral lessons are taught at every turn.

Communitarians sound like liberals because they worry about the poor rather than about the business climate. Because most of them share a left or social-democratic background, they still see the Democratic Party as the likeliest vehicle for their ideas. But their philosophy is not liberal in a strict sense at all; liberalism is an Enlightenment philosophy that develops political arrangements out of the notion that individuals are born with rights.

Communitarians downplay both individuals and rights in favor of social obligations and the collective good. As Stephen Holmes argues in *The Anatomy of Antiliberalism,* a brilliant dissection, communitarian thinkers like Alasdair MacIntyre and Roberto Unger unwittingly recapitulate the views of fascist theorists such as Carl Schmitt and Giovanni Gentile.

In its soft-core version, communitarianism hardly raises a totalitarian specter. Communitarians who are engaged in real-world politics do not really reject individualism or rights. They just try to supplement them with a sense of the common good. In championing expressions of *community,* a word which, Holmes notes, they invest with "redemptive significance," they do not actually propose reverting to antiliberal rules. For example, communitarians are deeply troubled by family breakdown. But they rarely argue for restricting divorce; that would violate their notion of individual rights. Ideologically, communitarians function as the antithesis of libertarians and a kind of left analogue to the Republican authoritarians. The difference is that where conservatives like Bennett and Reed want to impose morality on others, communitarians long for others to impose morality on themselves voluntarily.

This halfheartedness often leaves communitarians looking like glib moralizers or worse. For example, in 1993 the communitarian self-promoter Michael Lerner won brief notoriety when Hillary Clinton borrowed his term "the politics of meaning." It was indeed a nice phrase. The problem was, neither Lerner nor the First Lady could explain what such a politics entailed. It was simply a way of radiating seriousness and concern without using the politically discredited vocabulary of welfare-state liberalism. It was a Democratic way of saying, as George Bush once put it, "Message: I care."

Bill Clinton has employed communitarian ideas more successfully, if sporadically. Amitai Etzioni, a Washington-based guru of applied communitarianism, has been among the president's freelance advisers; William Galston, another of their number, was a senior policy adviser until 1995. Under this tutelage, Clinton endorsed such proposals as weapons sweeps of public housing projects and requiring the use of a computer chip that would give parents more control over their children's television viewing.

These are good, practical ideas, and communitarianism is not without its uses for the Democrats. A kind of modern, ecumenical ethics, it seems to help liberals get over their hangup when it comes to talking about morality. It also serves as a useful counterweight to the excesses of civil libertarianism. But it is no solution for the Democrats, because it does so little to sort out the pressing issue of government's responsiblities. Communitarians provide a better formula for moral exhortation than they do for collective action. Their ideas make for a fine Sunday sermon; where they fall down is in drawing up Monday's program. Beyond a few rather obvious suggestions, like trying harder to collect child-support payments from delinquent fathers, their big policy ideas are mostly naive efforts to promote ethical behavior through tax incentives.

Communitarians make a case that many of America's fundamental problems are not at root political ones. Man's inhumanity to man is not the product of government, and government cannot solve it. But once you have reminded yourself of that truism, there is still the question of what we can do through our political institutions. And on that point, communitarians don't have much to offer; their whole philosophy points away from government.

The Democrats' Dilemma

The most conscious and convincing attempt to synthesize these various critiques and strategies for liberal renewal was Bill Clinton's 1992 campaign. Clinton understood each of these approaches and borrowed selectively from them in an attempt to forge a new majority coalition.

In his earliest efforts as a presidential candidate Clinton followed the New Democratic recipe. He began by "inoculating" himself against the viruses of cultural politics. On crime, Clinton was an exponent of the death penalty. When it came to defense, he asserted his readiness to use force when necessary. Instead of truckling to the interest groups in the primaries, he made symbolic attacks, the most celebrated of which was his denunciation of black militancy at a meeting of the Rainbow Coalition. He couched programmatic ideas like national service and welfare reform in the language of values; he supported Osborne-style reinvention of government. Clinton supplemented his New Democrat side with economic populism. He spoke passionately against "trickle-down economics" and declared himself on the side of a middle class that was, as he put it, "getting the shaft." He drew upon economic nationalism as well. Campaigning in the rust belt, Clinton decried the unfair trade habits of the Japanese. Nor did the reactionary liberals go begging; Clinton selectively championed social programs for which a strong case could be made, such as Head Start. He flavored the mixture with a sprinkling of communitarianism.

Many disparaged this amalgamation as hypocrisy. From a political point of view, however, it was a display of tremendous acumen. Clinton managed to generate genuine enthusiasm among groups that are usually more inclined to flay each other than fight the Republicans. He blended seemingly incompatible parts into a workable whole.

In 1992 the soufflé rose. Vital to the accomplishment, however, were a couple of random factors: the 1991 recession and Ross Perot. The more typical conditions of American politics are still the two-way race and the growing economy. In normal circumstances, there is no reason to think even a Democrat who splits differences as skillfully as Clinton will have much of a chance. In 1992 Clinton negotiated an artful victory. He did not, however, concoct a new recipe for his party, one that could be used again by him or someone else. And once he took office, the task of turning an electoral coalition into a governing one proved nearly impossible.

The display of harmony among Democratic factions lasted for about a week into Clinton's presidency. Shortly after his inauguration, when he moved to allow gays into the military, he angered the New Democratic critics of cultural liberalism. When it became clear he did not have the congressional votes to pass his reform, Clinton backed off, upsetting a key interest group. In emphasizing deficit reduction in his first budget, he infuriated both New Democrats, who thought it should be an overriding goal but found his attempts insufficient, and paleoliberals, who felt spending cuts violated Democratic "values." In proposing health care reform, he alienated both those to his left, who wanted a straightforward government-run program, and those to his right, who worried about the expansion of big government. Is it any wonder his middle is a muddle? A Clinton who walked a clearer ideological line would be less frustrating to his sympathizers; he would have more permanent allies and antagonists; he would get more respect. There is no reason to think he would have a larger base of support.

After the 1994 election, Clinton's first instinct was to proclaim that he was a Republican before the Republicans; he boasted of his efforts to reduce the federal workforce and diminish the deficit. He too was a believer in less government, he said, though *less* less government than conservatives wanted. In the next six months, Clinton ran through all the familiar ideas again, frenziedly trying to see if anything would help. He tried an economic populist position of denouncing favoritism for the rich; he brought the country to the brink of an economic nationalist trade war with Japan; he retreated to reactionary liberalism in defending Medicare, Social Security, school lunches, and student loans. In a rambling address at Georgetown, he gave a précis of communitarian themes. Then, in an instant, he was a New Democrat again, overriding his own reactionary liberal proposal with a balanced budget plan. Watching Clinton in 1995 was like seeing a familiar movie on fast-forward. The various Democratic factions increasingly criticized him less for rejecting their views than for being preposterously inconstant.

Clinton's attempts to explain his philosophy of government on a more abstract plane have been less than lucid. In a *Newsweek*

colloquy with Gingrich in March 1995, Clinton shrewdly sum-
marized the contradictory views of most members of the public
about government—they want less of it, but they want it to solve
problems tomorrow. Yet his own view reflected the same contradiction. "I've understood for nearly twenty years that there's not a
big government solution to every big problem," Clinton noted,
elaborating on the many programs he had reduced or eliminated.
"But it is equally wrong to say that government is the source of
all our problems and will only make things worse."

Fine, but what *is* the role of government? "We have to
develop a role for government as partner, constantly committed
to creating opportunity and making people feel safer," Clinton
asserted. This is a version of the idea he expressed during his
campaign and at the 1992 Democratic Convention as the "New
Covenant"—government should help those who help themselves, enlarging opportunity instead of dispensing benefits. At a
speech at a Democratic National Committee fund-raiser during
the summer of 1995, Clinton touched on this idea again, repeat-
ing that his party believed the purpose of government was "to
help people make the most out of their own lives."

The New Covenant expresses what Clinton's long-time
adviser Dick Morris calls a "transactional" approach to government. Government does for those who do something for themselves and their country. It is an appealing notion, because it
suggests aid to those at the bottom of the social ladder while moving beyond the paleoliberal concept of government as redistribu-
tor of income and dispenser of compassion. The New Covenant
model, which draws on both communitarian and New Democratic ideas, holds out the hope of refiguring currently unpopular
interventions on a more popular, moral, and productive basis. It
remains Clinton's best idea, his most important contribution to
the project of liberal renovation.

But Clinton, for some reason, has never been able to get the
idea across with sufficient force or clarity. Hardly anyone understands what the phrase *New Covenant* means. An even more serious problem is the way he has applied the New Covenant

philosophy in practice—or more accurately, has failed to apply it. When it came to welfare reform, the effort that was to express most clearly the New Covenant idea, Clinton did not follow out the implications of his theory. The New Covenant suggests a changed bargain for the poor; help, but only in exchange for work. Clinton made this point often at the rhetorical level. But his plan, when it finally arrived in 1994, only tentatively applied that notion. Clinton was afraid to propose a major public jobs program, afraid to spend much on poor people, even with a plan that emphasized the right values. In 1995 he endorsed a Senate Republican bill that demanded responsibility but failed to offer any appreciable job opportunity in exchange. In so doing he dropped the New Covenant for the No Covenant.

A final difficulty is the conflict between the New Covenant idea and Clinton's other promising idea, reinventing government. Rego means a reduced public workforce. But a New Covenant approach necessitates more, not less, bureaucracy. One of the few things government can do simply and efficiently is mail out checks. If it wants to create opportunities and enforce responsibilities, it undertakes a more challenging and expensive task. A New Covenant government offers the moral advantage of reciprocity, but that comes with increased costs and complexity.

The way around this conflict is to make the case for more paternalistic government in a few areas where we badly need it. Instead, Clinton has backed away from the hard choices implied by the New Covenant, turning it into a kind of intellectual mush. What he argues for devolves into a kind of Goldilocks philosophy. How much government should we have? Not too much. Not too little. Just enough. In 1996 he is trying, as he did in 1992, to gloss over the party's internal differences—in the interest of Democratic survival this time, not just for the sake of victory. He may carry it off, especially with the help of an independent candidate. But in doing so he will not have solved the fundamental problem any more than he did the previous time.

Democrats can still be the party of government—ambitious, assertive, and aggressive. But to do so they must break with their recent past. They have to admit past mistakes and commit themselves to clearing away the debris of past failures. They must accept new limits on the federal government and offer a clearer sense of the nation's priorities. Most of the party's leaders in Congress, though, seem to think of power as a kind of birthright, which will return to them if they bide their time and stick steadfastly to the old certainties. They haven't come to grips with what majority support for the Republican revolution means. They know they've been grounded, that they won't be creating any big new programs in the next couple of years. But they think, as Peter Jennings infamously commented on election night in 1994, that the voters simply had a "temper tantrum."

Reactionary liberals are right that Republicans are bound to trip up. But until the Democrats themselves articulate a view of government that commands respect, they will not recover their lost position. The public may turn to them out of unhappiness with the conservative attack on government, but it will not be a real mandate or an endorsement of their views. The Democrats will remain a party of rejection, not affirmation. To choose an incendiary analogy, they will resemble the reformulated communist parties in post-communist Eastern Europe. When they win it will say nothing about them and everything about fear of the alternative. Without substantial change, Democratic victories will be few and far between, temporary and also hollow.

Chapter Five

RESURRECTING GOVERNMENT

Government is the most precious of human possessions; and no care can be too great to be spent on enabling it to do its work in the best way; a chief condition to that end is that it should not be set to work for which it is not specially qualified, under the conditions of time and place.

— ALFRED MARSHALL, *Industry and Trade,* 1919

IN A 1995 *Atlantic Monthly* article entitled "Really Reinventing Government," Peter Drucker notes the paucity of systematic thinking about the content of government action as opposed to its form. His point is well taken: classical political philosophy is more interested in ideal structure than in what functions a properly constituted government should undertake. But Drucker's own proposal is simply to apply business logic to the public sector. He suggests we rank government's efforts according to how well they work, testing results as a corporation would and dumping the poor performers. On this basis, he nominates for extinction most of what government does today, including welfare and the fight against drugs. "To reform something that malfunctions—let alone something that does harm—without knowing why it does not work can only make things worse," he writes. "The best thing to do with such programs is to abolish them."

Such obtuse analysis glides past every interesting question in its rush toward an absolutist conclusion. Certainly, there are problems government is ill suited to address. But it makes no sense to take an episode of failure, even conspicuous failure, as proof of futility. It is true, to be sure, that government is not now accomplishing certain tasks effectively. Welfare and the war on drugs are obvious examples. What has been discredited, however, is merely the way in which we have pursued these problems. No one has convincingly demonstrated that government is intrinsically incompetent when it comes to preventing destitution or mitigating the social and personal damage caused by narcotics. The casual assumption that government has failed because an ugly problem persists is naive. There is little way to know where we would be without such efforts unless we quit them, which seems too great a risk for the sake of an experiment.

The libertarian throws up his hands at the interplay of social evils and imperfect solutions and says it is no concern of the state's. But the liberal answers that government not only has the potential to better society, it has a moral obligation to do so. As Richard Hofstadter writes, what united and distinguished the first modern liberals, the members of the Progressive movement that dominated politics in the years between 1900 and America's entry into the First World War, was their disposition toward activism. "They argued that social evils will not remedy themselves, and that it is wrong to sit by passively and wait for time to take care of them," he notes in his introduction to a collection of Progressive writings. "They believed that the people of the country should be stimulated to work energetically to bring about social progress, that the positive powers of government must be used to achieve this end." The legatees of the Progressive tradition have fallen out of favor in many respects, but the public, in the depths of its cynicism, has never rejected their broad aspirations for a more humane and equitable society. It has not traded liberal values for libertarian ones.

Liberals lost the support of the nation not because of their ideals but as a result of the flawed way they put them into practice.

Too often they let enthusiasm get the better of common sense. The progressive-liberal tradition cannot recover so long as it means supporting futile or counterproductive efforts just because they are attempts. A liberalism that wants to be popular again must free itself from sentimentality and adopt a stance of hard-headed pragmatism. It must recognize that "social progress," however noble an idea, is not, and cannot be, the primary function of government. Some evils may simply transcend our ability to remedy them. We have a Samaritan's obligation to try to mitigate the worst. But we must take care not to bankrupt ourselves or neglect primary obligations like defense and public safety in the pursuit. In the United States, the revolt against government will end when liberals reassess their priorities and begin to act sensibly in pursuit of the right ones. Faith in government is not given, it is earned. Restoring public trust is a matter of creating the kind of government that deserves it.

The good news is that most of the groundwork for such a renovation exists within the liberal tradition. Building a workable public activism is not a matter of starting from scratch but rather of recovering and renewing lost principles. For a historical source, it is useful to look back before the New Deal and Great Society to the Progressive movement. In its original incarnation, progressivism offers a needed corrective to liberalism as it has come to be defined by the Democratic Party over the past few decades. Looking back to the old Progressives, we find a liberalism without a century's accretion of bad habits, without mawkishness or excess. We find a practical, democratic approach to bettering the country. By reviving progressive ideas, liberals can fit themselves for governing again. By resurrecting the term, we can indicate a break with our recent past and our link to an older tradition.

Though they were preoccupied with social maladies, the disposition of early-twentieth-century Progressives was confident and optimistic. The leaders of the movement were broad thinkers who rejected the ingrained parochialisms of both parties and approached problems from a national and global point of view. Progressives were our first real free traders, our first internationalists, our first environmentalists, and our first consumer advocates. In an era of self-interest and special interest run amok, they asserted the national government's responsibility for the welfare of the entire polity. Progressives embodied the philosophy, as Walter Lippmann put it in the title of one of his best books, of answering a period of drift with an assertion of mastery.

The Progressive movement arose not at a moment of crisis, as did the New Deal, but rather at a time similar to our own—one of growing aggregrate prosperity accompanied by increasingly glaring disparities. Where the original Progressives were preoccupied with the social and economic dislocations of an emergent industrial order, today's liberals are concerned with a similar kind of painful transition, to a postindustrial society. The Progressive era was also a period, like our own, characterized by disenchantment with the two major parties. In the words of the Progressive Party platform of 1912:

> Instead of instruments to promote the general welfare, they have become tools of corrupt interests which use them impartially to serve their selfish purposes. The deliberate betrayal of its trust by the Republican party, the fatal incapacity of the Democratic party to deal with the new issues of the new time, have compelled the people to forge a new instrument of government through which to give effect to their will in laws and institutions. Unhampered by tradition, uncorrupted by power, undismayed by the magnitude of the tasks, the new party offers itself as the instrument of the people to sweep away old abuses, to build a new and nobler commonwealth.

Whether a third party is the appropriate vehicle for New Progressives is a matter beyond this book's scope. But the Progressive Party's spirit, its willingness to break with long-established patterns and traditions, is a major part of what liberals now require. In that platform of 1912, one glimpses the confident nationalism and assertive moralism that characterized the movement at its apogee. Those too are attitudes we need to recapture.

The principles liberals need to reassert today are, of course, not merely those of the Progressives. Ironically, much of our task is the antithesis of what they were about. Where the old Progressives confronted the problem of an insufficient government, the public sector we have inherited is perhaps insufficient in a few areas but more often excessive and ineffective. Government shrinkage is essential to our renewed vigor. But even here, the Progressives can help, by supplying a conception of limited activist government. That may sound to us like an oxymoron, but in the years before World War I, it was the only kind of activist government imaginable. The Progressives conceived of expanding collective power in an era when limits were still a precondition, when older priorities remained in place, and when common institutions were stronger than they are today. They built upon that foundation. We must rebuild it.

Liberalism with Limits

Chapter 2 looked at how government lost the public's trust. Conservatives see the disenchantment as rational and wish to deepen it. Liberals consider it irrational and think it can be reversed at the level of public relations. The new progressive thinks it grows out of real flaws and real failures, and that we can reverse it only through substantial change. Such a project must go far beyond "reinventing" government. Nor is it sufficient to prove that we are willing to get rid of a ridiculous program now and again. Rather, liberals must learn the habit of restraint. Simply stated, we must embrace the practice of limits in the public sphere.

Limited government is the essence of the liberal tradition and an integral part of the American idea. Under the Articles of Confederation, the thirteen colonies lacked sufficient authority to provide for their common needs. The Founding Fathers sought to devise a democratic power that could more effectively "promote the general welfare." At the same time, they were concerned that a new form of government might degenerate into a new form of tyranny. As Madison wrote in *The Federalist,* Number 10, "a passionate majority" might "sacrifice to its ruling passion or interest both the public good and the rights of other citizens." The Constitution attempts to balance the need for power with the risk of abuse by means of self-constraint. The framers thought a limited and democratic government would be stronger than the unlimited, undemocratic kind because of the citizen cooperation it could call upon.

Early constitutional government was by no means libertarian, but it was severely limited in practice. "In all the American republics the central government is only occupied with a small number of matters important enough to attract its attention," Tocqueville wrote of the Jacksonian republic. "It does not undertake to regulate society's secondary concerns, and there is no indication that it has even conceived the desire to do so." As Alfred Marshall might have said, because Americans viewed their government as precious, they took care not to apply it to tasks for which it wasn't suited. This belief in a strong, limited government, a government indeed stronger for its limits, remained an innate national possession through the expansion that followed the Civil War and into the early years of the twentieth century.

Progressivism is often viewed as a departure from the tradition of limited public power. In reality, however, Progressives did not advocate unbridled growth in government. They were motivated by the need to control a new kind of power, the private might of industrial gigantism. At the turn of the century, this force seemed so strong as to threaten the state itself. In response to it, Progressives asserted the need for a government that could cage the new beast and protect citizens from its ravages. But they remained deliberate and cautious in using the federal tool. "This, I know, implies a policy of a far more active government interference with social and economic conditions in this country than we have yet had," Theodore Roosevelt acknowledged in the first of his "New Nationalism" speeches of 1910. "But I think we have got to face the fact that such an increase in governmental control is now necessary." Roosevelt's expansion was reluctant; there was no alternative to stronger government.

During the New Deal, liberals began to lose touch with the old habit of limits. As historian Otis Graham notes in his book *An Encore to Reform,* the surviving Progressives objected to FDR's eagerness to use federal power. They missed in him the hesitancy to deploy government with which they credited both his cousin Theodore and Woodrow Wilson. Because of FDR's readiness to employ coercion, many of the Progressives compared him to Stalin, Hitler, and Mussolini. Walter Lippmann's suspicion of the centralized-planning efforts of the New Deal grew until 1937, when he portrayed it in *The Good Society* as a form of "gradual collectivism," a radical departure from the liberal tradition.

There was a measure of truth in the observation. At the time Lippmann was writing, Roosevelt was proposing his ill-fated plan to pack the Supreme Court with additional justices in order to pass legislation that violated widely accepted limits on federal power. His administration included officials who were entranced by the power of illiberal regimes. Some New Dealers fell easily for the fallacy that modernity required centralized planning along with the dedicated service of Platonic guardians, experts and technicians like themselves (indeed, as a younger man, Lippmann was susceptible to this notion himself). Roosevelt never dabbled in antiliberal superstition but was given to a species of optimism that tended in the same direction. By the end of his administration, the notion of a federal government limited to a narrow and specific set of concerns had become a historical artifact. In 1940 Roosevelt spoke of what he called the Four Freedoms, which artfully blurred positive and negative liberty as no president had ever done before. In a 1944 speech he endorsed the idea of "a second Bill of Rights under which a new basis of security and prosperity can be established for all." America seemed to owe its returning G.I.s no less. But in promising to take care of them, FDR perhaps unwittingly initiated a process by which all problems increasingly came to be seen as public responsibilities.

Roosevelt's drift toward paternalism supports Theodore Lowi's contention, in *The End of Liberalism,* that the New Deal settled the long-standing question of the scope of government power "by establishing the principle for all time in the United States that in a democracy there can be no effective limit to the scope of governmental power." But once FDR set this precedent, it still took some time for the idea of comprehensive government to diffuse through society. Lowi marks 1961 as the year that what he calls the Second American Republic was born, the moment when consensus enveloped Roosevelt's vision. "This new attitude at its most general level can be described as an eagerness to establish and maintain a national government presence in all aspects of social and economic life," he writes. To Lowi, the problem with the Second Republic is that it cannot practically arbitrate among conflicting interest-group demands. Instead it yields to all, growing into a vast administrative amoeba.

By the time Lowi's book was published in 1969, many liberals were arguing openly for an unlimited state, albeit cast in the more attractive terms of the Swedish model. "The Democratic Party must henceforth use the word socialism," wrote John Kenneth Galbraith in his 1970 book *Who Needs the Democrats.* "It describes what is needed." While we never moved toward the redistributive example of northern European countries, we did develop in the sixties and seventies a habit of heavy-handed interference in private affairs, a "nanny state," as the Thatcherites liked to call it in England. In the seventies a Republican president imposed wage and price controls, enforced by a pay board and a price board; a Democratic one lowered the highway speed limit from seventy-five to fifty-five.

The first step in the recovery of public trust is for liberals to rediscover the joys of limited power. Restraining government does not have to mean keeping it entirely out of the economic or moral spheres or forgoing all policies that smack of paternalism.

But it does mean knowing when to stop, even in pursuit of valid social goals. It means a return to the old Progressive reluctance to use the federal government. It means an ambition to diminish harm, not to eliminate it. If that sounds vague, here are five specific practices new Progressives can adopt in pursuit of limited government. Call them the five habits of highly effective liberals.

1. Accepting Risk

In the old days, risk was part of life. The hazards of poverty, unemployment, and disease might be mitigated and alleviated by government but not eliminated. But in the 1960s and 1970s, the moderation of the Progressives was supplanted by an unarticulated sense that government was responsible for ensuring a pervasive condition of health and safety throughout society. Henry Fairlie noted this change in respect to the space program. When three Apollo astronauts were killed in a launchpad fire in 1967, there was no question of abandoning the program. The occupation was understood to be an inherently risky one. By contrast, the *Challenger* disaster of 1986 halted manned space exploration for a period of years. Under the new mind-set, the federal government was responsible for every hazard that might be named. If members of the public faced dangers—knowingly or unknowingly, willingly or unwillingly—it was up to Washington to Do Something about it.

This should not be remembered as one party's legacy. In the late sixties and early seventies, Democratic Congresses passed, and Republican presidents proudly signed, open-ended laws that regulated everything under the sun. A chart in the 1979 second edition of Lowi's book maps the administrative explosion of the early 1970s under presidents Nixon and Ford. In those years we adopted legislation to deal with such problems as toy safety, egg safety, workplace safety, fish safety, port and waterway safety, boat safety, car safety, medical safety, consumer product safety; unsafe drinking water; the risk of poisoning; the dangers of lead, pesticides, noise pollution, water pollution, and consumer fraud;

the transportation of hazardous materials; violations of privacy; and unscrupulous leasing practices.

A case might be made for each of these as a legitimate exercise of federal authority—the people doing collectively what they cannot do for themselves individually. But taken together in a short space of time, they constituted a threat both to liberty and common sense; they turned liberals into what P. J. O'Rourke calls Safety Nazis. The reductio ad absurdum was the 1984 Democratic platform's expression of concern about match safety. Part of the problem here is using government as first recourse instead of last resort. Liberals failed to recognize that gains in safety can often be won by consumer pressure on the private sector. To take only one example, airbags now come as standard equipment in most American and foreign automobiles, not just because Washington mandates them but because consumers want and willingly pay for them. There is sometimes no alternative to regulation, but the other options should be exhausted first.

In using government to attack risk, liberals have generally been unwilling to address honestly the trade-offs involved. The goal of the Occupational Safety and Health Act of 1970, for instance, was "to assure so far as is possible every working man and woman in the nation safe and healthful working conditions and to preserve human resources." The Consumer Products Safety Commission was created the same year to reduce "unreasonable risk" from household products. Workplace and product safety are surely valid undertakings—areas where government ought to force some reduction in economic output in exchange for protection. But how much? The only truly safe coal mine is a closed coal mine; the only safe chain saw is no chain saw. But Congress isn't about to drive whole industries out of existence. Instead, it declares absolutist goals and leaves the details to the bureaucracy, which must accommodate political reality. This leaves liberals overextended as usual—promising to prevent risks that they have no hope, and in truth no realistic intention, of ever eliminating. By making the federal government responsible for vagaries of life over which it can have no real control, liberals enhance their reputation as hopeless utopians instead of winning credit for measured gains.

Nor did they learn their lesson in the 1970s. Lately, liberals have moved to attack risk in ways that might have seemed absurd even then. One sees this in the mind-set that considers every military death a matter for investigation; in the requirement to make flame-retardant children's pajamas followed by the banning of flame-retardant chemicals as carcinogens; and in laws mandating asbestos removal that have imposed huge costs in exchange for statistically insignificant long-range health benefits. If you are more afraid of fire than cancer, tough luck.

The most prominent manifestation of this trend lately has been the crusade to regulate cigarettes out of existence. The ongoing decline in smoking should be seen as one of the success stories of limited government. The Surgeon General's warning, adopted in 1964, was part of a traditional public health campaign based upon simple discouragement of an unhealthy practice. It aimed at persuading members of the public, regarded as rational beings, not to smoke. It was cheap and it worked. But it didn't end all smoking. This provoked liberal legislators, led by Rep. Henry Waxman of California, to treat smokers as wards of the state. In the summer of 1995 President Clinton took a giant step in that direction by accepting a recommendation from FDA administrator David Kessler to classify nicotine as a dangerous drug on the basis of its addictive properties.

Few things contribute more to the liberal caricature than using such excuses to regulate irrationality. A child cannot grow up in the United States without being instructed in the dangers of cigarettes. Yet people continue to smoke because they find it pleasurable, sexy, or whatever. It is part of human nature to make bad choices. We need to accept them. That is not to say that freedom is incompatible with a modicum of paternalism; cigarettes should be kept away from minors. The government ought to propagandize relentlessly against smoking, as it does. But citizens of a free country have a right to do things that are dumb, even dangerous to themselves, so long as they don't harm others.

2. *Underpromising*

We ought to ban the following words and phrases from political discourse: "no American," "every American," "always," "never," and "cure," "solution," "end," and "guarantee." Part of government's bad name today stems from its habit of making offers too good to refuse and impossible to fulfill. In politics, overpromising is worse than simple promise breaking because of the disrepute into which it casts the entire system. When a specific pledge is broken, a politician has broken it and can be held accountable in the next election. But when politicians commit themselves to the fulfillment of broad goals, and those goals go unmet, public trust is damaged. The enterprise of government itself appears to fail, even in circumstances where the goal was unrealistic and politicians might otherwise be credited with a limited success. If we want to reduce cynicism, we must forswear the habit of visionary overreach that feeds it.

The unrealistic promise has been a staple of politics since elections were invented. But it is LBJ who deserves the greatest share of blame for the modern liberal habit of rhetorical inflation. Perhaps he was ruined by the delicious experience of ending segregation, which really was that rare thing, a quick and complete government victory. But whatever the reason, his grandiosity got the better of us. The paradigmatic episode was Johnson's effort to assist the poor, which he couched in the most immoderate rhetoric. It was "an unconditional war on poverty" that would break "the cycle of poverty," assure every American a decent home, end welfare, and train the poor to compete for jobs. A war, let alone an "unconditional" one, suggests a fight to the finish in which there is a victor and a vanquished. Poverty does not work that way. It will always exist, in one form or another. In any case, the metaphor fails to describe the ill-conceived and underfunded effort that followed from Johnson's words. Judged on its own terms, as Ronald Reagan used to quip, we fought a war on poverty and poverty won.

Had Johnson defined his program as a set of ambitious attempts to alleviate misery—which is what the War on Poverty really was—the actual results would probably have been no different. It might have been tougher to sell the program to the public, but it would also be harder to cite programs that in fact reduced the American poverty rate by half as a basis for opposing renewed efforts. Only if it was a war did we lose it. Unfortunately, politicians have a short time horizon and habitually choose the instant gratification of avowal over the deferred satisfaction of fulfillment. Senator Edmund Muskie, the author of the Clean Air Act of 1970, declared as its intention "that all Americans in all parts of the country shall have clean air to breathe within the 1970s." Only against that absolutist standard can our efforts to control air pollution be judged a failure. Again, the problem has not been limited to Democrats. Among George Bush's goals were 100 percent drug-free schools in which every child begins each day "ready to learn." Early in his presidency, Bill Clinton declared as goals a nation in which every student has the opportunity to go to college, every child is immunized, no American goes without health insurance, and welfare is replaced by work. These were aspirations he had little hope of fulfilling during his presidency even in the event of astounding success.

Liberals should have a dream. But when it comes to specific programs, friends of government ought to frame them in terms of the seriousness of our problems and the extent of the effort they intend to make. Politicians should promise only as much as or less than they realistically think they can deliver: more Americans going to college, fewer without medical coverage. Clinton might have proposed welfare reform aimed at seriously reducing the number of Americans trapped in a cycle of dependency. The realism of an aspiration ought to be a selling point. It is a measure of respect for the public to think it might be willing to support the efforts of government on the basis of reasonable expectations.

3. Saying Good-bye

In a healthy government, programs would not accumulate like junk in the attic. They would be sorted out in an annual spring cleaning. It seems almost too obvious to explain why some programs need to be terminated. Efforts should expire when they have accomplished their missions, as well as in cases where they don't work well enough to justify continuation. In a world of limited resources, old programs need to get out of the way to make room for new ones. Instead, we have bureaucratic forts that endure long after their wars have ended. There are programs still on the books that were designed to help electrify rural areas and to ensure the military supply of helium, which hasn't been a strategic material since World War II. Such absurdities are the ultimate proof that Weber, not Marx, understood bureaucracy; its nature is to expand, not wither away.

Gore's National Performance Review has done an impressive job ferreting out surviving absurdities like the wool and mohair program and the Interstate Commerce Commission as well as mountains of silly rules (though even these can be diabolically difficult to eliminate). But progressives need to be bolder, leading the charge beyond obvious waste to functions that are beneficial but expendable. Do we need a separate system of veterans' hospitals? Farm supports? Public television subsidies? There are also some new programs that have demonstrably not worked, like Clinton's immunization plan, which was based on the faulty assumption that parents weren't vaccinating their children because of the cost. Zeroing out a program shouldn't depend on demonstrating that it is worthless. Every bit of government spending helps somebody. What liberals need to recognize is that if we want to try new programs someday, we have to get rid of old ones first. We should begin by shooting a few hostages, to show how serious we are about limiting government.

Wherever possible, programs should be self-liquidating, through sunset laws and sunset clauses. A set expiration date fosters a mission mentality in place of a bureaucratic one. At the very least, programs should have to plead their cases for renewal on a regular basis. The assumption today is that government programs continue until someone notices their fruitlessness or extravagance. Instead, we should frankly assess every few years whether all public efforts merit continuation. On that basis, we would have gotten rid of the Tennessee Valley Authority, still with us in the 1990s, decades ago.

One politically powerful formula is to connect future government expansion to government shrinkage. Robert Shapiro of the Progressive Policy Institute expresses this idea well in a paper called "Cut and Invest." Shapiro identifies $265 billion in budget savings over five years, much of which falls under a category he dubs "corporate welfare." Sixty percent of those cuts, he argues, should simply be savings that go to reducing the deficit. The rest he would dedicate to a program of new public investments— spending on education, training, infrastructure, and targeted tax breaks that can be expected to have long-term payoffs. This is an attractive combination. Progressives should get in the habit of always marrying the repeal of the old to the promulgation of the new. In a government with limits, slimming and growth go hand in hand.

4. Making Congress Do It

Theodore Lowi thinks the Second Republic was made possible by the New Deal–era abandonment of something called the nondelegation doctrine. The nondelegation doctrine is the principle that Congress cannot pass its responsibility for making law to anyone else. For 150 years, the Supreme Court understood Article One of the Constitution to say this; on that basis it threw out key pieces of the New Deal in several cases, the most famous of which was *Schechter Poultry Co.* v. *United States* in 1935. The court ruled that by giving presidential appointees power to fix prices and set marketing and production quotas, Congress was engaging in an unconstitutional handoff of its power. After his reelection in 1936, FDR proposed his infamous court-packing bill to change the court's mind. The bill failed, but the court was intimidated. Soon thereafter, it began siding with the New Deal. Roosevelt joked he had lost the battle but won the war.

Though *Schechter* was never overturned, the nondelegation doctrine became a dead letter. It was replaced by what Lowi calls "unregulated regulation." As a labor-saving device, delegation did for legislators what the washing machine did for the 1950s housewife. Government now had the ability to penetrate every nook and cranny of American life in a way that was simply impossible before. In his book *Power Without Responsibility,* David Schoenbrod examines the Clean Air Act as a case study of modern regulation. It was politically impossible for most legislators to vote against such a noble goal as clean air, and few did. But likewise, few desired to face the trade-offs involved in actually reducing pollution. Thanks to delegation, they found a way around the problem. With the 1970 law, they passed to the EPA the burden for defining what "clean" meant. They forwarded the bill for attaining the to-be-determined standards to the states.

This was no solution. Before long, erstwhile champions of the act were trying to prevent the EPA from implementing it. Members of the New York delegation who had voted for the law marched across the Brooklyn Bridge to protest a ruling that the city had to impose tolls on its bridges and tunnels to implement it. The EPA soon succumbed to pressure to reverse key interpretations of the act. But the cost of delegation isn't just ineffective law and endless litigation; it's unfairness. The broad public goes unrepresented inside the regulatory agencies. Only moneyed interests, who can afford lawyers and lobbyists, operate effectively within such labyrinths. By evading hard choices about what pollutants to restrict, to what degree, and at what economic cost, Congress created a situation that was good for no one except a parasitic class of Washington lawyers and lobbyists. Evading choices also feeds what Lowi calls "the nightmare of administrative boredom," as democracy moves from the floor of Congress into the minuscule typography of the *Federal Register.*

Defenders of delegation assert that modern life is too complicated to do without it. How could Congress possibly have time to
deal with the myriad details handled by all of the regulatory
agencies that now exist? Though this assertion is superficially
plausible, there's no real evidence for it. Delegation is itself time
consuming. Under the prevailing model of "narrow" delegation
Congress still has to pass intricate legislation giving the agencies
detailed instructions about how to go about their regulating. It
deals with this problem by developing its own network of spe-
cialists, who are fully capable of writing law in place of guidelines
for making law. Members of Congress and their staffs stand to
save millions of hours they now spend navigating the regulatory
thicket on behalf of constituents. In any case, stealing time from
such essential duties as showboating at committee hearings and
groveling for campaign funds might not be such a bad thing.
Sound election finance reform would free up enough of the average congressman's schedule to do away with delegation and
spend more time with the kids as well.

Reasserting the primacy of congressional decision making
would mean better rules. Congress can't draft four thousand
pages of OSHA regulations, so it would be encouraged to move, as
Schoenbrod recommends, toward a simpler model. It might, for
instance, tax energy usage instead of regulating the efficiency of
every appliance. Ending delegation would act as a check on government's ability to grow ad infinitum. By rejecting it, progressives
can provide a practical answer to the libertarian-inspired conservative assault on all regulation. They would declare themselves
responsible regulators, in favor of only so much law as Congress is
able to make itself.

5. Fixing a Size

People who complain about big government object not just to
bigness per se but to the potential for growth without end. Progressives should recognize that this is a legitimate concern, and
answer it by accepting a theoretical limit. Of course, it is naive to

think that government's power is strictly determined by its size. In wartime, a minimalist state can consume a nation's entire economic output. And government has the ability to regulate in ways that create the conditions of a command economy without technically taxing or spending a large share of anyone's income. But the aggregate is still meaningful; in a democracy like ours, the size of government, figured by such traditional measures as share of GDP and number of employees, provides a rough approximation of power.

Our federal government spends approximately $1.5 trillion a year, roughly 22 percent of the national economic output. It takes in only about 19 percent. The missing 3 percent is our annual budget deficit. State and local governments add another 11.5 percent of GDP, bringing government's share of the economy in at just over a third. To give a sense of perspective, in 1979 that number was still under 30 percent, in 1948 less than 20. In Scandinavian countries, by comparison, the government's share of the economy has been as high as 72.5 percent. In Sweden, the heftiest, that number is now down to the high 60s. A government that large is bound to undermine incentives and invade private space. It raises the specter, successfully exploited by George Bush in 1988, of a social democratic state with excellent social benefits— accompanied by high unemployment, epidemic tax evasion, and limited potential for growth.

A first step toward assuaging suspicions that we are moving toward an all-consuming government is to balance the budget. Democrats need to do so for both political and substantive reasons. In political terms, it is only within the context of a balanced budget that the public is likely to approve affirmative government again. In economic terms, the debt absorbs too much private capital. In public policy terms, the growing cost of interest on a growing national debt is crowding out the entire domestic discretionary budget. In theory, we don't need to have a balanced budget every year; in a recession, countercyclical stimulus is a useful tool. It can also make sense for a government to borrow for investments, as opposed to current consumption. Even Madison allowed that "debts may be incurred with a direct view to the interest of the unborn as well as of the living." But we need to reestablish a baseline of balance before those nostrums will be meaningful again. The economy has existed in a state of Keynesian overstimulation for nearly twenty years. We've discovered that we can't just have a few drinks. Given the reality of the problem, progressives must forswear spending beyond our means, period.

The next thing to do is to indicate how great those means ought to be. There is no tipping point at which we become Swedish. But we have to draw the line somewhere. One-third of GDP, a bit more than the government now takes in (but slightly less than what it spends), seems intuitively reasonable. New Progressives could say that in peacetime the activist government they favor is slightly smaller than the one we have now, and that they intend for it to stay that size—forever. That's not to say that government can't spend less, just that under normal circumstances it won't spend more. With this rule, government could no longer grow at the expense of the private sector. To develop new programs, we would need either to draw down other efforts, discover new efficiencies, or benefit from economic growth. This gives government an incentive to foster economic expansion; it must increase the size of the pie if it wants to do more.

Republicans had a version of this idea in the 1970s. Milton and Rose Friedman mention it in their book *Free to Choose* as one of seven desirable constitutional limitations on government. It was a neglected plank in Ronald Reagan's 1980 economic program. The logic behind a constitutional maximum size was that self-discipline had become impossible. In office, the Reaganites proved their own point by failing to show any. But a constitutional amendment would be unwise. We need to be prepared for wars and other crises we can't foresee. Instead, New Progressives should simply propose a principle: that in normal times they favor a federal government that consumes no more than 22 percent of the national income, and a government that at all levels absorbs a maximum of one-third. More than can be bought for that price we won't try to buy.

To be a Swede means your government takes two-thirds of what the nation produces and gives it back in the form of generous, universal benefits. If you are an American your government claims only half as much. With that, it tries to save you from disaster, but your prosperity depends to a greater degree on luck and ability. If Democrats adopted a fixed limit, Americans would understand that one party wasn't working to turn them into Swedes.

Progressive Priorities

American liberals have grown Swedish in another way as well: by failing to think clearly about how to order public responsibilities. They talk and act as if the social welfare state were the essence of government, the military an unfortunate historical artifact. Otherwise shrewd people fall easily into this inversion, which badly damages liberal credibility.

The National Endowment for the Arts deserves more money, not less, *Time*'s art critic Robert Hughes contends in a Gingrich-era defense of culture funding. "So why not give it one-quarter the cost of a B-2 each year—$550 million?" Liberals can't seem to shake this cliché: butter is so cheap, guns so dear. The problem is that the two things are incommensurate. You can't weigh the one in terms of the other. Of course we shouldn't waste money on defense, as Republicans seem determined to do. The B-2 is a boondoggle, to be sure, and since the end of the Cold War a largely gratuitous one. But that argument needs to be considered separately, on its merits, and in the context of meeting military needs. Defense is a necessity, the most basic one of all. Arts funding is a luxury. We need to provide adequately for the former before talking about the latter.

Progressives need to demonstrate that they recognize the distinction. It is not enough to accept grudgingly that the armed forces and police are important. We need to affirm these functions as the lifeblood of good government, more important, if one had to choose, than Social Security, school lunches, and arts funding. This ranking makes practical and moral sense. It is also a democratic reality; only when citizens are secure in their rights and their property are they likely to have an appetite for helping the disadvantaged, let alone subsidizing the Santa Fe Opera. What progressives should say is that the United States is a prosperous enough country, thank goodness, to take care of the necessities, maintain a welfare state, and afford a cultural life as well.

Republicans have a more instinctual dedication to the security functions of government. But their priorities are skewed too. When they get beyond the basics, conservatives tend to select their missions far more capriciously than liberals do, supporting, for instance, space exploration and subsidies for rich farmers, but not job training or antipoverty programs. One of the ways for progressives to answer the Republican attack on government is to establish our own, more compelling priorities. We need to assert in clear, easily comprehensible terms our view of government's functions and then convince the public that it is right. With apologies for the immodesty of the exercise, I propose that we rank the responsibilities of government according to three distinct tiers:

• The first tier is a free government's primary obligation: to safeguard the rights of its citizens: freedom of speech, of religion, of association, of movement, of property, and the right to democratic and legal process. These fundamental rights imply a duty on the part of government to create and preserve the basic conditions under which they can be exercised. That means providing for the common defense, maintaining public safety (a function traditionally performed at the state level), and administering the rule of law. These functions require revenue, so the first tier implies not only a currency and monetary system but taxation as well. If our government aspired to go no farther than this level, the result would be a minimalist state, a libertarian skeleton. If it failed at these first-order responsibilities it would be no government at all but rather anarchy.

• The second tier involves basic collective purposes: developing the means for individuals to pursue their own interests freely and fairly, and for creating the conditions under which the economy can grow. Functions at this level include safeguarding the environment, protecting public health, providing infrastructure for communication and transportation, supporting a system of universal education, and maintaining public institutions such as parks and libraries. The last few of these functions again belong to the states by tradition. Tier two suggests at least a rudimentary welfare state: one that takes care of injured veterans, provides a safety net for the physically and mentally incapacitated, and affords some provision for the destitute. Shortcomings at this level do not delegitimate a government as the breakdown of first-order responsibilities does. But a government that fails here fails profoundly, even if it does not violate the social contract.

• The third tier is affirmative government. It is aspirational and inevitably somewhat experimental in nature. It is the attempt to advance broad national purposes, to fulfill what the Progressive writer Herbert Croly called the promise of American life. It means the amelioration of the nation's particular problems and an effort to mitigate the ravages of an unfettered market economy. The third tier begins with efforts to combat social ills like the exploitation of labor, unemployment, poverty, illiteracy, discrimination, and inadequate housing and health care. It encompasses efforts to ease economic dislocations affecting the nonpoor, and to spur upward mobility. Also included in this category are efforts to promote advancement in science and medicine, enhance the cultural and intellectual life of the country, and promote democracy and fight problems like overpopulation and environmental degradation abroad. It is important to bear in mind that many of these aspirations may not be fully achievable. Success at accomplishing them must be measured against a different standard than tasks on tiers one and two. Progress is bound to be incremental and relative, a never-ending project.

These tiers correspond, very roughly, to the growth of American government over time. The first was erected in theory by the Articles of Confederation. But the system failed to authorize a means to raise revenue sufficient to defend the country and made no provision for the second-order collective undertakings that would allow the country to grow. The Constitution enabled the second tier, which filled in during the nineteenth century, though there remained, of course, massive exceptions to first-order ideals: slavery and the absence of universal suffrage. The third tier began around 1900, with the presidency of Theodore Roosevelt, and has continued through the twentieth century. It covers most of what liberals still aspire to today.

The boundaries of the third tier also imply a fourth: nonpriorities or invalid functions of government. In that category belong various efforts that don't serve national purposes in any obvious way. Here we find subsidies to profit-making enterprises, benefits that are simply expressions of regional or special-interest power, and welfare for people who don't need it. Such unjustified provisions have always been with us, but since the end of the Second World War they have developed on a massive scale.

Republican antigovernment rhetoric notwithstanding, there's little real dispute about tiers one and two. There is even a bipartisan consensus that government must take on some third-level tasks, such as Social Security and Medicare. But a question soon arises about trade-offs within tier three. The rubric of affirmative government subsumes the two great issues of the moment: the economic stagnation of the American middle class and the far more serious problems of the underclass.

In a period of straitened circumstances, it seems something should have to give. And if we opt to help the worst-off, won't we drive members of the middle class farther from supporting affirmative government and the party that believes in it? Liberals have by and large come to absorb the conservative critique that the interests of the American middle and lower classes diverge and that Democrats have been on the wrong side. That's why hardly anyone in the party talks directly about helping the poor anymore. The theorists, from economic populists like Stanley Greenberg to the centrist New Democrats, all buy into the notion of such a dichotomy and say they want to help the struggling "middle class."

But the opposition between middle- and lower-class interests is false for several reasons. First, the widespread belief that the federal government now helps the bottom instead of the middle is an enormous distortion of reality. Programs and policies that benefit middle-class people dwarf those that help the poor. Social Security costs about $350 billion a year; AFDC, $18 billion. Medicare, which goes to all senior citizens, cost $160 billion in 1995; Medicaid, which goes to the poor, $88 billion. The mortgage tax deduction is worth $60 billion, rent subsidies $22 billion. The American voter habitually takes his own benefits for granted while attributing to "government" any program that assists someone else. Progressives need to remind those who complain bitterly about the raw deal they get from Washington of all they overlook. In this sense, we should be resolutely antipopulist, explaining to middle-class voters how government does help them.

Second, the ongoing fiscal crisis has left a sense that we must employ some form of triage in deciding whom to save. But when it comes to broad policy choices, there is no reason we can't help the middle class and the poor at the same time. There is plenty of tier four, superfluous government to dump before worrying about triage on tier three. Some quick arithmetic: a means test that would reduce but not eliminate Social Security benefits for those with incomes over $32,000 gets you $60 billion a year. Cutting corporate welfare and limiting the employer write-off for health care insurance brings in another $40 billion. A $20,000 cap on the home mortgage interest deduction is good for another $10 billion. That's $110 billion a year not being used for deficit reduction. The most expensive proposals for reforming welfare and for boosting stagnant middle-class wages have each been estimated to cost $50 billion. If we find something that works, there's money to pay for it.

This is doubly true if we proceed according to an experiment-and-expand model. In addition to being financially prudent, this approach comports to common sense, especially when it comes to the economic problems of the middle class. Our country is undergoing a transformation from an industrial to a postindustrial economy. The nation as a whole will be better off for this evolution, and we have no real choice about it in any case. The problem is that, as during the industrial transformation of the late nineteenth century, many people suffer in such a process. They lose jobs, their incomes drop, and even those who end up doing better exist in a state of perpetual insecurity. Unfortunately, we have only hypotheses about how to mitigate this harm. One possibility is revising labor law to bolster unions, which doesn't cost government directly. But the truth is we don't know enough to justify costly new universal programs. Government-assisted retraining schemes, for example, have yet to demonstrate meaningful improvement in wages. Should we happen upon something that does work, the investment will pay for itself over the long term. The same is true when it comes to programs for those at the bottom of the heap. If any of the ongoing experiments with welfare lead to a solution that succeeds well enough to be nationalized, such a program would be self-limiting in terms of cost. Reform that actually turned public charges into taxpayers would eventually pay for itself many times over. In the meantime, we can try everything plausible and still have change left over for the NEA.

Programs to help the underclass can also appeal to the middle class on the basis of values. Welfare reform based on the New Covenant idea—a plan that requires work and makes it available—will be expensive. But it will not be indulgent. Many poor people, and their advocates, will be unhappy with it. When it comes to convincing the middle class, that's a political strength.

But the final and most important reason that the interests of the poor and the middle class are not opposed is that their fates are intertwined. Crime, the demise of public spaces, and the low quality of much public education are crises for both groups.

Government may make marginal improvements but cannot substantially affect what New York mayor Rudolph Giuliani calls "quality-of-life" issues without relieving the poor. We can't increase public safety in a fundamental way without improving opportunities for the people who commit most crimes. Public spaces can't be made agreeable so long as homelessness goes unaddressed. The same holds true in other areas. To many middle-class Americans, the prospect of falling down the economic ladder means tumbling into a moral and material abyss. The country would reap an enormous psychological dividend if downward mobility meant only having less money while retaining a decent level of comfort.

What makes life bearable for the lower class has a ripple effect on everyone else. It makes us feel better about being Americans. But because members of the middle class lack options available to the rich, such as private schools and exclusive neighborhoods, they stand to gain especially. The higher floor advocated by Democrats promises them more than the raised ceiling of the Republicans. Members of the middle class benefit more from the earned income tax credit, even if they make too much money to qualify for it, than they will from a capital gains tax cut. The former means that if they lose their good jobs and have to take crummy ones, they will still have enough to survive. The latter means that if they become extremely wealthy someday, they will pay lower taxes. Trickle-up thus promises the vast majority more than trickle-down. The Republican strategy is to unite all who are not poor on the basis of self-interest. The progressive answer should be to draw together all who are not rich on the basis of interest as well as common humanity.

A CLEARER VISION of public priorities doesn't entirely sort out government's role. There remains the age-old question of federalism: once we decide what to do with limited resources, which government should do it? Much of the political debate today is a wrangle over the splitting up of rules, responsibilities, and revenues among Washington, the states, and their subsidiaries. The struggle over the intergovernmental division of labor contributes to disenchantment by fostering a culture of buck passing. The mayor of New York says the state should pay for the city's Medicaid program as other states do; the governor says it can't pay because the federal matching formula is too low; Congress won't change the formula because it deems the city too generous. Everyone leaves the debate with an excuse for failure. Confusion over responsibilities also leads in many cases to a debilitating search for national answers to what are inherently local matters, like education. The best way to improve education is to get involved locally, not lobby for more Title I funds.

The Republican solution to the problem is devolution. It, along with tax-cutting, remains the essence of Reagan's legacy to the G.O.P. Reagan's argument was deeply disingenuous from the start; the Reaganites were less indignant about the states' being deprived of their rightful roles than they were eager to dump responsibilities. Letting states decide whether to fund social programs would be a neat way to get rid of them. In trying to outdo each other promising to liberate states from the federal yoke, today's Republican leaders cement the alliance between libertarians who want less government and authoritarians who want less federal interference with state authority. The contradiction between these viewpoints shows up in the inconsistent application of federalist principles. When it comes to law enforcement, a function unequivocally belonging to the states, Republicans champion an active and paternalistic federal role.

Democrats tend to be more consistent in their pro-federal stance. Their New Deal–era bias in favor of a strong national role was underscored by the experience of the civil rights movement. In that instance, their disposition had a sound basis in fact. But after many southern states broke with their racist traditions, the liberal prejudice against them lingered. State officials were still seen as narrow-minded bigots; real change could be accomplished only at the national level. Our last two Democratic presidents, Jimmy Carter and Bill Clinton, both former southern governors themselves, have pulled the Democrats away from this mentality. But the party still stands for an augmented national role. Clinton sees Washington's job as helping, rather than restraining; he has tried to one-up the Republicans by giving the states more financial help in fighting crime.

One liberal who has tried to rethink the federal-state relationship is Alice Rivlin, Clinton's budget director. In *Reviving the American Dream,* a book she published shortly before joining the administration, Rivlin argues that since the federal government is overburdened and can't raise taxes in a responsible way for political reasons, it should shift some functions to the states. She wants state governments to take primary responsibility for education, welfare, and a new economic agenda aimed at raising productivity. The national government, she argues, should take care of defense and foreign policy and handle social insurance.

Rivlin is right about the benefits of dividing tasks. Making clear which jobs are federal, which are state, and which are local would point civic energies in the right direction. But social policy, if we want it to work better than it does now, cannot simply be the job of states. Without federal involvement, the differences between rich and poor states are likely to grow more extreme, just as differences between rich and poor people widen in the absence of labor law, progressive taxation, and a minimum wage. Without a federal role in housing, welfare, and other programs for the disadvantaged, states will be tempted to compete negatively by providing fewer and lower-quality services. If Washington isn't paying, each state is better off encouraging its poor to move elsewhere. Rivlin comes to grips with this reality when she examines health care, which she thinks must be a federal responsibility.

Progressive federalism means accentuating a dynamic whereby states compete at social innovation and at better programs and services, rather than over who can provide the least. When it comes to social policy, why can't the federal government be the orchestra conductor, remaining focused on the totality while the sections play their separate parts? This is essentially the system we have now; it recognizes that programs must be implemented

184 • IN DEFENSE OF GOVERNMENT

at the state level but that in terms of the major areas of social policy, Washington has an important job overseeing experiments, collecting objective data, celebrating successes, and encouraging the spread of policies that demonstrate results. Sometimes it must reject schemes that are nationally harmful. Washington's leverage is money. When it comes to social programs, states are autonomous and have the right not to participate. But if they want financial support, they can reasonably be asked to operate within certain rules.

The Civic Space

Once liberals learn to accept limits, establish a valid set of priorities, and add a moral component to the safety net they provide for the poor, they will have solved their biggest problems. They will no longer threaten deeply held American values. But there will still be the lack of trust in government that arises from the decline of political institutions. Among the most obvious deficiencies of late-twentieth-century American democracy are a system of campaign finance and a culture of influence peddling that allow moneyed interests undemocratic power, a system of taxation that baffles the ordinary citizen, and a degraded conception of public service. These are prolific breeders of discontent, apathy, and cynicism.

Democrats and Republicans share responsibility for institutional decay, but progressives have the most pressing need to reverse it. People who mistrust the system aren't likely to be interested in its new fruits. Any future program of activism hinges on systemic reforms that will re-create the sense of a level playing field in our politics. Because we aspire to use government in a more ambitious way, new progressives have an imperative to clean it up.

Here again, the old Progressives can help to light our way. Their original impulse was anger at political corruption and abuse of the public trust. Some of the specific concerns that animated them, like the power of urban bosses, railroads owning senators, and the tyranny of the trusts, are now historical artifacts. So too are many of the reforms for which they struggled: the direct primary, the Australian ballot, the initiative, referendum, and recall. But much of the broad Progressive critique is surprisingly applicable after the passage of nearly a century. Listen to David Graham Phillips, writing in the April 1906 issue of *Cosmopolitan* (then a rather different kind of magazine):

> The greatest single hold of "the interests" is the fact that they are the "campaign contributors"—the men who supply the money for "keeping the party together," and for "getting out the vote." Did you ever think where the millions for watchers, spellbinders, halls, processions, posters, pamphlets, that are spent in the national, state, and local campaigns come from? Who pays the big election expenses of your congressman, of the men you send to the legislature to elect senators? Do you imagine those who foot those huge bills are fools? Don't you know that they make sure of getting their money back, with interest, compound upon compound?

Subtract the eloquence and you have the daily plaint of Common Cause. Or consider the words of Woodrow Wilson, denouncing the tariff lobby in 1913: "It is of serious interest to the country that the people at large should have no lobby and be voiceless in these matters, while the great bodies of astute men seek to create an artificial opinion and to overcome the interests of the public for their private profit." That, minus the gravity, was the essence of Ross Perot's 1992 campaign.

The original Progressives understood that for government to be legitimate, politics must be a fair contest. "If our political institutions were perfect, they would absolutely prevent the political domination of money in any part of our affairs," Theodore Roosevelt said in 1910. While realizing that perfection was impossible, the Progressives set their aspirations high. Recognizing that lobbying and political spending couldn't be banned in a free society, they argued for "publicity," or what we now call disclosure, as the tool of first resort. The Progressive Party platform of 1912 proposed disclosure as a remedy for both lobbying and campaign contributions. Shame was the principal mechanism to force change.

While the outrages of political corruption are gripping stuff, the mechanical side of political reform is a numbing subject. That too has not changed since the Progressive era. As Herbert Croly wrote in his 1914 book *Progressive Democracy,* the push for political reform grows "impoverished and sterile as soon as it becomes divorced from a social program." Reform has to be for something, "connected to a political ideal," in Croly's words. In his day, that ideal was a program of government activism and expansion. The irony is that today we need progressive reform to help us shrink and rationalize government, to make it an effective tool again. By taming those interests organized around special privileges and benefits, reform promises us less government, not more. New Progressives understand that for government to become activist again, it must first retrench and consolidate.

Thanks to the Supreme Court, which defined spending as speech in *Buckley* v. *Valeo,* comprehensive reform is largely impossible. But we can still eliminate the most flagrant abuses by moving toward voluntary public financing of congressional campaigns. When it comes to lobbying, we need rules for disclosure with genuine penalities for noncompliance. If those measures don't work we can try something else. What's needed above all is a reassertion of the morality that the early Progressives brought to bear on politics. The slogan that advertises Saturn cars should hang over the halls of Congress: We treat everybody the same. This is a matter of morality more than law. It means abiding by voluntary spending limits and not working to unearth new loopholes in campaign financing restrictions. It means shunning revolving-door, hired-gun lobbyists. More would be accomplished by our next president's simply refusing to appoint influence peddlers to high office than by any set of legal restrictions on ex-officials.

The problem of public integrity isn't just the practice of profiteering at the highest levels. Progressives need to restore an older idea of national service to the lower ranks of government as well. Once again, the situation is replete with historical ironies. The age of reform was preoccupied with the vestiges of the spoils system—the corrupt overpoliticization of public sector work. In its place, the old Progressives wanted a more efficient and honest bureaucratic system, what they called "scientific administration." Today our problem stems from an excess of apolitical independence. In the absence of democratic control, public service bureaucracies have become dysfunctional. Employees don't have to answer for failure. To restore public service we need an infusion of accountability. In practical terms, this means removing at least one of the two layers of insulation that protect government workers: the civil service or public employee unions. Unions make a better choice.

This step will be infinitely difficult for liberals, since public employees are the most loyal of Democratic constituencies. According to Gordon Black, a pro-Perot pollster, nearly half the delegates at the 1992 Democratic convention worked for government in some capacity. But the separation is essential. More than any other force, unions have turned public service into self-service. According to a 1994 story in the *New York Times,* it took an average of forty months and cost $200,000 to fire an incompetent teacher in New York State. Unions clog the arteries of government. They stand in the way of meaningful reforms, raise costs, and prevent the cutbacks that are required for new growth. Government service is different from other kinds of work. It has different attractions, different rewards, and different protections. Other workers have unions but no civil service rules. Let government workers have their rules but no unions.

What we will offer public servants in exchange is a windfall in respect. If America succeeds in developing a civil service closer to either the European model or our own historical example, working for the government will become far more appealing than it is today. During the Roosevelt and Kennedy administrations, a government job offered the opportunity to participate in a great adventure. We can't simply summon that mood back into being. But we can strive to create the kind of government that the best people want to join.

A final political institution in desperate need of reform is our tax system. Here the fundamental problem is complexity, which creates opportunities for unfair advantage. Conservatives offer a tantalizingly simple reform: the flat tax. The ease and seeming impartiality of such a system are deeply appealing. A flat tax would eliminate the loopholes that sustain a small nation of lobbyists, lawyers, and accountants. It would operate on the democratic assumption that everyone pays a fair share to support our common institutions. But the Republican scheme is also heavily biased in favor of the rich, who would pay no tax on dividends, inheritance, or capital gains. In the name of simplicity the flat tax would do away with progressivity.

Recognizing the value of a straightforward system comprehensible to all, progressives should offer the alternative of a simple graduated income tax. There might be three rates—say 20, 30, and 40 percent. Loopholes would be phased out over time, which would mean the end of economic distortions caused by perverse incentives. The landscape of the future would not grow cluttered with superfluous high rises built for the sake of tax shelters. With this system, as with a flat tax, returns might well be filed on a postcard. And with the size of government fixed, the rules could remain highly stable over time. Such a plan would also give progressives a tax cut of their own to tout: reducing or eliminating Social Security withholding, a crushing, regressive burden that also functions as a tax on job creation.

The National Interest

Nationalism is not a word that comes easily to liberal lips. Democrats instinctively shrink from its small-minded and super-patriotic connotations. It is a disposition that has motivated too many historical crimes, inspired militarism and colonialism, and led to a river of bloodshed. It has also provoked an extreme over-reaction. Rejecting any sense of a national identity, many on the left have adopted a multicultural view that sorts the country into racial and ethnic compartments. They emphasize what makes us different, not what we have in common.

This not only promotes a balkanized society, it undermines the very programs multiculturalists want to support. Without some sense of collective purpose, everything government does simply provides an advantage to one group at the expense of another. Absent nationalist fellow feeling, government is an "it" that works for "them." With it, government can again become an "us." Nationalism doesn't have to imply bigotry; it can mean the simple assertion of a common American identity, a sense that for all our diversity we are part of a unified culture with certain shared values, interests, and aspirations. It is a way to cast efforts to help afflicted groups as urgent collective undertakings and not just favors to special interests.

The best guide to the recovery of this notion is the Progressive thinker Herbert Croly. If Croly is a familiar name today, it is for two achievements: founding the *New Republic* in 1914 and publishing *The Promise of American Life* in 1909. A book whose current alternates between rhapsodic eloquence and impenetrable verbosity, one that is moving and maddening at the same time, *Promise* is probably the greatest single work to come out of the Progressive movement. Faced with the explosion of private commercial power that so troubled his contemporaries, Croly set himself the task of justifying the kind of public action needed to check it. In so doing, he laid the foundation stone of modern liberalism.

For Croly, the promise of American life was inescapably material: "a promise of comfort and prosperity for an ever increasingly majority of good Americans." Yet at the time he wrote, that ideal seemed to be receding. What Croly called "the social problem" was growing and could only be addressed, he argued, by a concerted deployment of national resources and attention. "No voluntary association of individuals, resourceful and disinterested though they be, is competent to assume the responsibility," he wrote. "The problem belongs to the American national democracy, and its solution must be attempted chiefly by means of official national action." Or, as he puts it later in the book: "The House of American democracy is again by way of being divided against itself, because the national interest has not been consistently asserted as against special and local interest."

Lately, *Promise* has attracted attention, not just from liberals searching for their roots, but from conservatives probing the source of the ideas they abhor. In an essay that leads off a recent volume published by the conservative Hudson Institute entitled *The New Promise of American Life,* Lamar Alexander blames Croly for devising a philosophy Alexander calls "governmentalism"—the assumption that government holds the solution to every problem. Though it may be worth pointing out that Alexander himself was no stranger to such an inclination before the antigovernment bug hit the Republican water supply, he is to be credited for choosing a worthy antagonist. What Alexander misses is the context in which Croly wrote. In the first decade of the century, the federal government performed only the barest minimum of essential tasks. To make the case for action on a broader scale did not imply unbounded activism. The idea of limits was not lost until decades later.

It is easy to pick out anachronisms that make Croly sound absurd or worse. He was obsessed, as were his contemporaries, with order and efficiency, and with the possibilities for a benevolent, scientific management of society. There is something a bit chilling in the quasi-religious faith Progressive intellectuals had in experts and rational planning. Croly was also a matter-of-fact racist, though he considered himself a friend to "the negro" and admired Lincoln beyond all compare. He saw colonialist expansion as a salubrious expression of national feeling. Yet none of this diminishes his great contribution, which was to locate the affirmative use of government in a historical tradition. What Croly convincingly demonstrates is that the Progressive assertion of responsibility for the public welfare was not an aberration but an approach firmly grounded in American tradition. As he put it in a later book, *Progressive Democracy,* "Progressivism is not a new birth of public spirit; it is a rebirth. It is not an awakening of public opinion to something novel; it is a reawakening. It is not aiming at an unprecedented vitalizing of democracy, but at its revival along traditional lines."

Croly's story begins with Hamilton, not Jefferson. Jefferson stood for the idea that the country's problems would take care of themselves. Hamilton, by contrast, though Croly thought him too mistrustful of democracy, stood for the idea of "an energetic and intelligent assertion of the national good." As secretary of the treasury, Hamilton proceeded on the theory that "the central government is to be used not merely to maintain the Constitution, but to promote the national interest and to consolidate the national organization." Croly arranged the rest of American history along the Jeffersonian-Hamiltonian split. Andrew Jackson and his followers opposed the development of a beneficial national organization out of a misguided egalitarian impulse. The Whig leaders Henry Clay and Daniel Webster were Hamiltonian federalists, but feeble ones. Lincoln was Hamilton's real heir, the second member of Croly's personal pantheon. As he writes: "No progress was made toward the solution of the slavery question until the question itself was admitted to be national in scope, and its solution a national responsibility." Recognizing this was Lincoln's great achievement.

The leader of his own day whom Croly most admired was Theodore Roosevelt. Roosevelt was in fact deeply influenced by *The Promise of American Life* and took from it the slogan of his postpresidential period, the New Nationalism. "Mr. Roosevelt has imparted a higher and more positive significance to reform," Croly wrote, "because throughout his career he has consistently stood for an idea, from which the idea of reform cannot be separated—namely the national idea." Croly saw Roosevelt as third in the trinity, a president almost as great as Lincoln.

The future of Progressive nationalism, Croly assumed, lay principally with Roosevelt's party, the Republicans, and subsequently with the Progressives. The Democrats, he believed, were incorrigible Jacksonians, too antagonistic toward the idea of "national organization" to be any help in developing it. Woodrow Wilson, a progressive Democrat pushing a program of federal consolidation, appeared to Croly not as the avatar of a great party reversal but merely as an aberration. Croly, who died in 1930, never lived to see how Wilson was to set a new pattern; how the party of Lincoln and Roosevelt was to degenerate into the champion of localism and stasis; how another Roosevelt would address "the social problem."

But Croly has made his posthumous home among the Democrats just the same. After Teddy Roosevelt and Wilson, his truest followers were Franklin Roosevelt, Harry Truman, and John F. Kennedy. These Democrats were consummate politicians who welded electoral majorities out of interested groups. But they never spoke to the country in terms of its factions. They led it as a nation. When they wished to move forward, the great midcentury Democrats addressed us as a single community, connected by mutual obligation, interdependence, and a sense of honor.

The decadence of the liberal ideal in the period since the Kennedy assassination is attributable to many things discussed in the preceding pages—the loss of limits, the confusion of priorities, the inflation of expectations, the decline of institutions, and the ebb of moralism in public policy. A no less central problem, however, has been the failing conception and expression of a unified nationality. Our three Democratic presidents since Kennedy have all had a sense of the concept, to be sure, but none has given adequate voice to it. They have failed to distinguish sufficiently between politics and government, between what's right for the Democrats and what's right for the country. They have all suffered from a tendency to regard the nation as an agglomeration of interested and aggrieved factions. This has something to do with the imperfect leadership qualities of those men who have come to occupy the White House, but also relates to the spread of a mind-set that regards uninflected sentiments like national purpose as anachronistic relics.

We may be surprised to see progressivism reemerge some-where other than the Democratic Party, just as Croly would have been surprised to see his ideas flourish there in the first place. But the tradition is bound to reappear. "We refused to leave the problems of our common welfare to be solved by the winds of chance and the hurricanes of disaster," Franklin Roosevelt said in his second inaugural address. That was more than a description of his first term; it was an exhortation. We have always been a country with problems. We have never been the kind that gives up on them.

CONCLUSION

Here's a story of the kind of government I'm talking about.

In the fall of 1960, a young woman named Vivian Malone applied to the University of Alabama's Mobile branch, where she wanted to study accounting. Because Malone was black, and Alabama segregated, her application was summarily rejected. Several years earlier, the NAACP Legal Defense Fund had won a court order admitting another African-American woman, Autherine Lucy, to the university. But Lucy's attendance drew a violent mob, and on the thinnest of pretexts, university officials expelled her.

Now the NAACP was ready to test the waters again, and Malone, who worked as a volunteer secretary in the organization's Mobile office, appeared as the perfect plaintiff. A straight-A student at Central High School, she was pretty, reserved, affable, and perhaps most important, brave. Detectives at the state Department of Public Safety, under orders to investigate black applicants for the purpose of searching out skeletons in their closets, were frustrated to find nothing on her. Malone's parents both worked menial jobs—her father as a maintenance man and her mother as a maid. They were hardworking people, committed to the civil rights movement and dedicated to creating a better life for their eight children. With the NAACP's backing, Vivian

Malone reapplied, this time to the university's main campus in Tuscaloosa. Joining her was another African-American, a track star named Ray Hood.

In May 1963 a federal judge ordered the admission of Hood and Malone. But then another obstacle presented itself. George Wallace had just been elected governor of Alabama on a pledge to stand in the schoolhouse door to block the entrance of any black students. "I am the embodiment of the sovereignty of this state," Wallace said, "and I will be present to bar the entrance of any Negro who attempts to enroll at the University of Alabama." Desegregation, according to Wallace, was like Prohibition, a social experiment that wouldn't work. Despite a court order enjoining him from stopping the students, the governor said he would literally stand in their way.

It fell to the Kennedy administration to enforce the court order against Wallace. Attorney General Robert Kennedy sent Nicholas Katzenbach, the deputy attorney general, to Alabama to make sure the students were safely admitted. The Kennedy administration hoped to avoid in Alabama the deadly violence that occurred at the University of Mississippi in Oxford the previous year, when James Meredith was forcibly registered. The Kennedy brothers also wanted to avoid arresting Wallace, who promised a quarter-million Alabamans at his trial. But above all the Justice Department insisted that the law be upheld and that desegregation go forward.

A famous photograph from the *Birmingham News* shows the scene of June 11, 1963. Facing the threshold of Foster Auditorium stands the rumpled patrician figure of Nicholas Katzenbach, arms awkwardly folded across his chest, a rolled-up presidential order sticking out of the pocket of his suit coat. A burly federal marshal stands behind him. Katzenbach is stooping toward Wallace, who occupies the center of the doorway and is flanked by state troopers in short-sleeve shirts and construction helmets. Wallace, who is wearing a microphone around his neck, pitches his chin forward in a gesture of defiance.

"I have here President Kennedy's proclamation," Katzenbach

said. "I have come to ask you for unequivocal assurance that you or anyone under your control will not bar these students."

"No," Wallace replied. The governor then stepped up to a lectern to read his prepared statement. "I denounce and forbid this illegal and unwarranted action by the central government," he declaimed. And he did not budge.

"From the outset, Governor, all of us have known that the final chapter of this history will be the admission of these students," Katzenbach said. "I ask you once again to reconsider." He was met by a stony silence.

Later that day, Katzenbach, backed up by the Alabama National Guard, with another three thousand army troopers on alert nearby, would compel Wallace out of the doorway so Hood and Malone could register. But for now, their way was blocked. So Katzenbach proceeded with his backup plan. Having secured keys to the dormitory room that would be hers, Katzenbach walked Malone to Mary Burke Hall. The situation was tense. Frank Rose, the president of the university, was cooperating with the Justice Department but insisted that such a step was madness. "There's gonna be a riot if you do this," he told Katzenbach. Undeterred, Katzenbach decided not only to install Malone at her dormitory, but to escort her to the cafeteria for lunch.

Let's let Wallace biographer Stephan Lesher finish the story:

After freshening up, Malone went to the cafeteria and entered alone. Rose had strongly cautioned Katzenbach to discourage Malone from dining with the white girls, at least until a few days had passed, but Katzenbach was adamant that she assert her equality as soon as possible. "I'm not putting that off one minute," he recalls telling Rose. "That's what's going to happen in the future, and it's going to happen right now." Watching from the cafeteria entrance, Katzenbach said that Malone took a tray and went over and sat down at an empty table—and in thirty seconds, half a dozen girls had gotten up and gone over.

That afternoon, JFK himself called the networks to request airtime. At 8 P.M. he went live to relate the events leading up to the admission of Malone and Hood, "two clearly qualified young Alabama residents who happened to have been born Negro." After telling the story, Kennedy began to plead the wider case to which he was himself only a recent convert. Everyone ought to have the same right to receive equal services, to vote, to enjoy the privileges of being in America, he said. But that was not the case:

> We preach freedom around the world, and we mean it. And we cherish our freedom here at home. But are we to say to the world—and much more importantly to each other— that this is the land of the free, except for the Negroes; that we have no second-class citizens, except Negroes; that we have no class or caste system, no ghettos, no master race, except with respect to the Negroes? Now the time has come for this nation to fulfill its promise.

Kennedy said he was going to ask for legislation giving all Americans the right to be served in public facilities. He would also ask Congress to become more deeply involved in the desegregation of public education and in the effort to protect voting rights. But only Americans, he noted, acting in their private capacities, could really make integration meaningful.

One of those watching the speech at home was Reverend Martin Luther King, Jr., who had been until that evening a persistent critic of the White House for failing to take a more aggressive position on civil rights. Surprised and gratified, King immediately wrote Kennedy praising the speech as "one of the most eloquent, profound, and unequiv[oc]al pleas for Justice and Freedom of all men ever made by any President."

Vivian Malone reminds us of a time when we believed in the federal government, when Washington seemed to be guided by clear moral principles and uncompromised leaders with a strong sense of purpose. In retrospect, the Kennedy brothers may not always have deserved that esteem, but in this instance they certainly did. In their conversion to the cause of civil rights, the Kennedys came to understand that there was no alternative to federal action. By intervening, they weren't just doing a favor to black Americans, they were serving the country as a whole. In the University of Alabama episode, Katzenbach and the Kennedys acted as politicians in the best sense of the term: ambitious leaders who brought a shrewd pragmatic sense to bear in pursuit of higher goals.

Though it is about success, Malone's story is also a moral fable about limits of government. The Department of Justice could get her through the schoolhouse door at Tuscaloosa, but it couldn't make her fellow students or her fellow Alabamans accept her. That required a change in people's hearts. In the cafeteria, Katzenbach had a chance to see that awakening take place. That is the most powerful part of the story, because it is about a change that good government inspired but could not force.

These days such straightforward purposes seem lost to us. There are no more unregenerate racists like Wallace to make liberalism's case. The federal government seldom has the opportunity to intervene so unambiguously on the side of justice. But the eclipse of the good fight is something of an illusion. There are conditions in this country every bit as bad as those in Alabama in 1963—perhaps worse. They are no longer caused by legal segregation or official discrimination, but they are part of its historical legacy. To those born into such a world, there may appear little practical difference. For the worst-off blacks, American life still has not fulfilled its promise.

Thanks in large measure to the actions of the federal government, blacks as a whole have made enormous progress in the past thirty years. To many African-Americans, the despair of the underclass is remote, as it is to most whites. But life in the ghetto remains a catastrophe that humbles our hopes and mocks our ideals. As Kennedy told a mostly white nation about its black minority that June 11, "I think we owe them and we owe ourselves a better country than that." Today America faces many problems that a renewal and rededication of national purpose might serve. But none is more important than the legacy of our past racial injustices. To address this crisis requires a profoundly different mood from the one that prevails at present. It demands bravery on the part of political leaders who must ask sacrifices from people who don't feel they owe any.

Liberals, who cracked up on the shoals of race once before, are not eager to sail those waters again. But more than anything else, racial progress is what we need liberals and progressives for. There is no alternative to action on a national scale; the illness cannot cure itself. The conventional wisdom that middle America won't stand for helping poor blacks needs defying. Reducing the size of the underclass would rain benefits on every segment of American society. It would improve public education, reduce crime, save cities, and restore our sense of ourselves. The difficulties are formidable. But so too is the progressive spirit, even amidst the clamor of reaction. Americans like the national character reflected in the story of Vivian Malone, in the actions of a wise, effective, and benevolent federal government. That kind of democracy can be ours again. But first we have to want it.

ACKNOWLEDGMENTS

Bill Goldstein gave me the idea for this book. My agent Rafe Sagalyn, my editor Jane Rosenman, and my research assistants Kate O'Hara and Alexandra Lange helped bring it to fruition. I am indebted to Malcolm Gladwell, Michael Hirschorn, Mickey Kaus, Michael Kinsley, Nicholas Lemann, Robert Lieberman, David Mehnert, Sara Mosle, and my brother Joseph Weisberg for reading my work in manuscript and sharing their insights. Kurt Andersen and Sarah Jewler generously indulged my absences from *New York* magazine. Joshua Liberson did a beautiful job with the jacket. Finally I want to thank my mother, Lois Weisberg, whose service to govenment inspires me and everyone around her, and my wife, Deborah Needleman, for all her love and all of her help.

INDEX